PEOPLES *of*
NORTH
AMERICA

VOLUME 3

Colonial America – Egyptians

GROLIER

About This Book

Peoples of North America is a survey of the North American population at the start of the 21st century: the ethnic groups who make it up, their origins, culture, and lifestyle. The 10 volumes of the encyclopedia are organized alphabetically and describe all ethnic groups, from Afghans to West Africans. The peoples include well-established communities, relatively recent immigrants, and indigenous peoples who survive in significant numbers. Other entries also cover immigration-related and crosscultural subjects, such as intermarriage, music, and race, to help you understand how different groups have contributed to shaping modern North America.

Each entry on a specific ethnic group explains who the people are and where they live, where they came from, how they lived in the past and how they live now, and their arts, culture, and politics. Fact files and maps show the states and cities where the major communities live today. The fact files also allow you to quickly find useful information, including population figures, immigration history, languages, dominant religions, typical jobs, national foods, typical names, famous individuals, and major community organizations. The statistical data are from the U.S. and Canadian censuses. Where no date is specified, the data are based on the latest available figures: the 2000 U.S. Census or the 1996 Canadian Census.

Entries on ethnic groups all contain a box listing useful websites. There are also special boxes giving detailed information about key people, events, places, cultures, or traditions. A "See also" box at the end of each entry points you to related articles elsewhere in the encyclopedia, allowing you to further investigate topics of interest.

The index covers all 10 volumes, so it will help you trace topics throughout the set. A glossary at the end of each book gives a brief explanation of important words and concepts, and a timeline provides a chronological account of key events in the history of immigration to North America.

First Published 2003 by Grolier,
an imprint of Scholastic Library Publishing,
Old Sherman Turnpike
Danbury, Connecticut 06816

© 2003 The Brown Reference Group plc

Set ISBN: 0–7172–5777–0
Volume 3 ISBN: 0–7172–5780–0

Library of Congress Cataloging-in-Publication Data

Peoples of North America
      p. cm.
   Includes indexes
   Summary: Profiles the native and immigrant groups that have peopled North America, focusing on the modes and monitoring of immigration.
   Contents: v. 1. Afghans-Bosnians – v. 2. Brazilians-Colombians – v. 3. Colonial America-Egyptians – v. 4. Emigrés and refugees-Guyanese – v. 5. Gypsies (Romany)-Irish – v. 6. Iroquois confederacy-local politics, Canda – v. 7. Local politics, U.S.-Native Americans, Southeast – v. 8. Native Americans, Southwest and Mexico-Puerto Ricans – v. 9. Quebec separatism-social mobility and race – v. 10. South Africans-World War II.
      ISBN 0-7172-5777-0 (set : alk. paper)
   1. Minorities – North America – Encyclopedias, Juvenile. 2. Immigrants – North America – Encyclopedias, Juvenile. 3. Ethnology – North America – Encyclopedias, Juvenile. 4. North America – Population – Encyclopedias, Juvenile. 5. North America – History – Encyclopedias, Juvenile. 6. North America – Ethnic relations – Encyclopedias, Juvenile. [1. North America – Population – Encyclopedias. 2. Ethnology – North America – Encyclopedias.]

E49.P467 2003
305.8'0097'03 – dc21

                                    2003042395

For information address the publisher:
Grolier, Scholastic Library Publishing,
Old Sherman Turnpike, Danbury, Connecticut 06816

Printed and bound in Singapore

For The Brown Reference Group plc
Academic Consultants: Donald Avery, Professor, Department of History, University of Western Ontario;
Margaret Connell-Szasz, Professor of Native American and Celtic History, University of New Mexico
Editors: Rachel Bean, Andrew Campbell, Dennis Cove, Felicity Crowe, Mark Fletcher, Lee Stacy
Designer: Dax Fullbrook
Picture Researcher: Becky Cox
Indexer: Kay Ollerenshaw
Managing Editor: Tim Cooke

CONTENTS

Colonial America   4
Cossacks   7
Costa Ricans   8
Crafts   10
Crime, ethnic   12
Croatians   14
Cross-border migration, Canadian   17
Cross-border migration, Mexican   21
Cubans   27
Cultural borderlands   30
Cultural mingling   33
Cultural retention   37
Czechs   42
Danes   45
Dominicans   49
Dress and costume   51
Dutch   54
East Africans   59
Ecuadoreans   63
Education   65
Egyptians   68

Glossary   70
Further reading   71
Immigration timeline   72
Set index   73

Education in the colonies

Much of colonial children's education took place at home. Parents taught their children basic skills such as hunting and cooking, and some took upon themselves the task of teaching their children to read and write. Formal schools were not widespread throughout the colonies, although some families joined together to hire teachers to run small schools. In the early 1600s the Massachusetts colony passed laws requiring parents to teach their children to read and, later, for communities to set up public schools. Many young people served apprenticeships through which they learned a trade with a master teacher.

A modern replica of the Mayflower, *which sailed to the New World in 1620, bringing the earliest colonists.*

The colonial era of American history began in 1607 with the first permanent English colony in America and ended with the start of the Revolutionary War in 1775. During those 168 years colonial America evolved from a small group of settlements governed by Britain into a united country capable of self-government.

After Christopher Columbus's arrival in America in 1492 Spain, Portugal, and France all staked claims in North America. Beginning in the late 16th century, the British also voyaged to North America, but England's first attempt to establish a colony at Roanoke Island in 1585 was unsuccessful. In 1607, under the direction of England's King James I, a group of 100 British colonists founded Jamestown, Virginia, the first permanent British settlement in North America. The Jamestown colonists faced many hardships, including disputes with the local Native Americans, bad water supplies, and inadequate food and shelter; but the colony ultimately survived.

The Pilgrim Fathers

The second British colony in North America was established at Plymouth, Massachusetts, in 1620. It was set up by the Pilgrims, a group of Puritans who left England aboard the *Mayflower* to escape religious persecution. The Pilgrims are most famous for the Mayflower Compact, a written agreement that established equal laws for all, which effectively paved the way for democracy in America.

When the British colonists arrived in North America, the continent was already home to many groups of Native Americans with highly developed cultures; historians estimate that indigenous inhabitants in North America numbered about 4.5 million in 1500. At first, Native Americans were willing to help the colonists, and trade thrived between the two groups. Soon, however, the colonists forcibly laid claim to Native American lands, first for agriculture and later for their precious reserves of gold and silver. Wars sporadically broke out between the two groups and eventually Native Americans were banished to reservations, often huge distances from their homelands.

America's Population Grows

From 1607 to 1775 a constant flow of immigrants came to America, and the population grew to 2.5 million. Almost all colonists came from Europe, mainly

Great Britain. They were drawn to America largely because they could not find work in their homeland, they sought freedom of worship, or they were eager to receive land that was readily available for free or for a low price. However, not all colonists arrived of their own free will. Orphans were sent from England to America, and English convicts were transported to the colonies to become servants. Scholars believe that between 10 and 12 million Africans were forcibly transported to North America between 1650 and 1850 to work as slaves. Stripped of their rights, they worked on European-owned coffee, tobacco, and sugar plantations in the Caribbean, and the farms and mines in the southern colonies. The plantation culture of the southern colonies differed from the economic and political culture of the northern colonies, which was centered on farms and, later, manufacturing that used free labor. Friction between the two systems ultimately led to the Civil War (1861–1865).

By the mid-1700s 13 colonies were founded along the eastern coast of America. They were the New England colonies of Massachusetts, Connecticut, Rhode Island and New Hampshire; the Middle colonies of New York, New Jersey, Pennsylvania, and Delaware; the Chesapeake colonies of Virginia and Maryland; and the Southern colonies of North Carolina, South Carolina, and Georgia. The landscape of the colonies varied greatly, ranging from the rocky coastal lands of New England and the rolling countryside and large farms of the Middle colonies to the tobacco farms of the Chesapeake area and the Southern colony plantations.

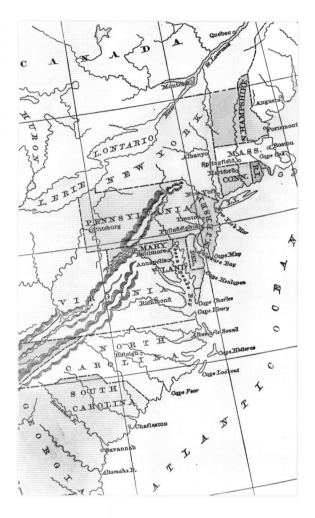

A 19th-century map of the 13 original colonies: Massachusetts, Connecticut, Rhode Island, New Hampshire, New York, New Jersey, Pennsylvania, Delaware, Virginia, Maryland, North Carolina, South Carolina, and Georgia.

Colonial Immigration Patterns

Immigrant patterns to these regions varied greatly. In the New England colonies immigrants were primarily English families, many of whom were Puritans. The Middle colonies were a land of many ethnic groups, including Dutch, Swedes, Finns, Germans, French, English, Scots, Africans, and Jews. The Dutch had an important place in the New York colony and Upper New Jersey colony, since they had first come to the area to build the early 17th-century trading outpost of New Amsterdam (located in present-day New York City). German-speaking people flourished in Pennsylvania, and those of the Quaker religion had a major presence in Delaware. The Southern colonies, particularly South Carolina, had a large number of African slaves and settlers from the Caribbean, and South Carolina became the only colony with an African-immigrant majority. The rural areas of the Southern colonies also drew many Scots-Irish and German farmers who had migrated from the Pennsylvania colony.

Modeling itself on English society, life in colonial America was largely structured according to three social classes—the gentry or upper class, the middle class, and the lower class. These class designations determined people's political rights, their style of dress, and how they worshiped. Unlike England, however, there was a high degree of social and economic mobility for most colonists, since a family could radically alter its social standing within a few generations through hard work and the acquisition of property.

The average American colonist lived a simple, hardworking existence. Most colonists lived in rural areas, and the vast majority of them were farmers. Crops varied according to climate and geography, and included wheat, corn, rye, rice, vegetables, and tobacco. Other jobs included fishing, whaling, lumbering, shipbuilding, brewing, silversmithing, glassmaking, and carpentry.

Colonial life centered on the family, and large extended families made up of several generations often lived in the same household. When the colonists first arrived in America, they made temporary shelters out of wood and mud. Later, they built modified versions of the houses they had left behind in their homeland. Because of the widespread availability of timber the average colonial home was a simple two-room frame building made of wood, with minimal furnishings and few decorative touches. Light was furnished by oil-burning lamps and fireplaces, which were also used for heating and cooking. Wealthier individuals had larger, more elegant homes. Colonial meals consisted largely of corn, squash, and wild game. Since they had few methods of preserving food, colonists often ate what was seasonally available. Dress was similar to English fashion of the day, with men wearing coats, vests, shirts, kneebreeches, and stockings, while women wore long dresses and shawls.

The Colonial Legacy

Rejecting the governmental legacy of Britain, the colonists developed a system of self-government built on democratic ideals. With slight variations the basic principle was that the property owners living in a particular area made political decisions. Within this system the majority of males in any community had a political voice in their community. As the American colonies further developed their own government, they began to resent and resist British rule from across the sea. This eventually led to the American Revolution and, ultimately, America's break from Britain.

See also

- African Americans (Volume 1)
- Dutch (Volume 3)
- English (Volume 4)
- French (Volume 4)
- Religion (Volume 9)
- Slavery (Volume 9)

A 19th-century impression of the arrival of (mainly unmarried) female settlers at Jamestown, Virginia, in 1621. They were recruited by the Virginia Company in England to improve morale and increase the colony's population.

Cossacks

The Cossacks ("Free Warriors") emerged on the steppes of southern Russia and eastern Ukraine, and were known for their horsemanship and military skills. At the end of the 19th century the Cossack homeland consisted of 11 semi-independent "hosts" or groups. All Cossack men served in the Russian army, protecting the empire from invasion and helping it colonize Siberia.

Many Cossacks died fighting the communists during the Russian Revolution (1917), and thousands fled to North America. Many who stayed in Russia were brutally repressed under the Soviet Union. After World War II more Cossack refugees emigrated. No accurate immigration records exist, but current estimates place the number of Cossacks and their descendants in the United States at 3,500 to 4,000.

Since the fall of the Soviet Union in 1990 a strong Cossack movement, supported by many Cossack Americans, has sought to reestablish self-rule within Russia and to revive traditional social structures. Just as the Cossacks see themselves as a special entity within Russia, they also consider themselves distinct from the Russian American community. Cossack folk dances such as the *kazachok* and *hopak* have survived. Their renowned choirs may be accompanied by traditional stringed instruments such as the *bandura* and the *kobza*.

Earliest immigrants

When the Russians colonized Alaska during the 18th century, some Cossacks were among the first settlers. The small number of Cossacks who arrived in North America during the 19th century included Ivan Turchaninov (John Turchin), who became a brigadier general in the Union Army.

See also

- Byelorussians (Volume 2)
- Emigrés and refugees (Volume 4)
- Russians (Volume 9)
- Ukranians (Volume 10)

Fact File: COSSACKS

Distribution

Portland | Woodburn | Chicago | Rhode Island
Cleveland
SOUTHERN NEW JERSEY
Los Angeles
San Francisco

Population

No accurate records of Cossack immigration exist, but estimates place those of Cossack descent living in the United States at 3,500 to 4,000.

Distribution

Many Cossacks settled the farming communities of southern New Jersey, with other groups in: Providence, Rhode Island; Cleveland, Ohio; Chicago, Illinois; Los Angeles and San Francisco, California; Portland and Woodburn, Oregon.

Food

Traditional Cossack fare includes boiled or grilled meats; *piroshki* or *varenyky* (dumplings); *blini* (fritters); and *golubtsi* or *holybtsi* (stuffed cabbage).

Jobs

Early immigrants were farmers and factory workers, worked in construction companies, or joined the military.

Community organizations

Kazach Amerikanskii Narodnyi Soiuz (Cossack-American National Alliance).
New Kuban Historical Society (New Jersey).
Cossack Web (artiom.home.mindspring.com)

Useful websites

World Factbook: Costa Rica
Basic information about the
country's geography, population,
government, and infrastructure.
(www.odci.gov/cia/publications/
factbook/geos/cs.html)

Costa Rica History
General article on the history of
the country
(www.interknowledge.com/
costa-rica/history.htm)

Costa Rica Home Pages
General information on National
parks, business, history,
economics, and art in Costa Rica.
(www.amerisol.com)

Tamales are corn husks filled with cornmeal dough and a mixture of fried meat and peppers. Tamales are one of several traditional Costa Rican holiday dishes.

The Costa Ricans, or "Ticos" as they are known, who migrate to the United States mainly live in the urban centers of either the greater Miami area of Florida or around Los Angeles in California. There are also Ticos in the New York and New Jersey metropolitan areas and in southern Florida. They are a conservative people who have integrated well into mainstream American society, mixing easily with other Hispanic immigrants. There are very few illegal Costa Rican immigrants.

The small country of Costa Rica lies on the Central American isthmus and shares borders with Nicaragua to the north, Panama to the south, and the Caribbean and Pacific oceans. It is about twice the size of Vermont and has a population of 3.3 million.

The reason for the comparatively small numbers of Costa Rican migrants and illegal immigrants is that Costa Rica is traditionally a stable country both politically and economically. Unlike other Latin American republics, Costa Rica made a peaceful transition to independence in 1821. Its population consists of more than 90 percent Europeans and some *mestizos* (people of mixed race), which means ethnic conflict has traditionally been avoided. Despite the many problems of its neighbors in Central America—with civil wars through the 1970s and 1980s—Costa Rica has continued to enjoy a peaceful stability.

Reasons for Immigration

Despite the political stability of the nation, a growing inflation rate and rising unemployment statistics have led some Costa Ricans to look for better economic prospects abroad. There are limited job opportunities in Costa Rica beyond tourism and the export of bananas, coffee, and other agricultural products. As a result there was a substantial increase in the 1990s in the numbers migrating to the United States, up from 57,661 in 1990 to 69,000 in 2000. As many as 35,000 American citizens—mostly retired—live in Costa Rica.

The earliest recorded arrival of Costa Rican migrants in North America is 1931. Since then a steady but small number of Costa Ricans have moved to the United States each year. On arrival they tend to settle in areas where an established Hispanic community already exists. For this reason both Miami and Los Angeles have drawn the largest numbers of Costa Ricans.

Costa Ricans bring with them many of their customs and traditions, but they tend to integrate over time. In the main they are eager to assimilate into the culture of both other Hispanics and their adopted country. Costa Rican Americans do not follow the traditional family patterns of home, where the father is in charge, and the extended family lives together. Typically in the United States both husband and wife work, unlike in Costa Rica, where many women stay at home. As a result of their increased financial status Costa Rican American women are more independent than their peers back in their homeland. Many Costa Ricans marry Americans and go on to adopt an American way of life, speaking English at home and eventually becoming U.S. citizens.

At holiday times and festivals Costa Rican Americans prepare special foods. One favorite is the Russian salad, or *ensalada Rusa*, which contains chopped-up potatoes, green peas, and fresh beets. The ingredients are mixed together with mayonnaise and sometimes hearts of palm. For holidays Costa Rican Americans also make tamales—filled corn husks wrapped in banana leaves. Fillings for the tamales vary but can include meat, potatoes, rice, garbanzo beans (chickpeas), olives, egg, and even raisins and prunes.

Arts, Culture, and Politics

At fiestas and other celebrations Costa Ricans enjoy listening to their favorite folk songs, which tell of their beautiful women and country. They also enjoy watching or taking part in their traditional courtship dance, called the *punto guanacasteco*. Many of the immigrants marry non-Costa Ricans and assume U.S. citizenship, with its attendant voting privileges.

See also

- Belizeans (Volume 1)
- Family patterns (Volume 4)
- Hispanic Americans (Volume 5)
- Panamanians (Volume 8)

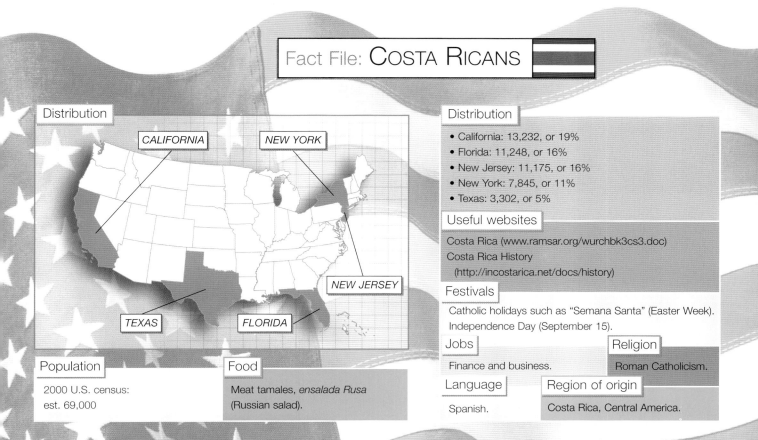

Fact File: COSTA RICANS

Distribution

CALIFORNIA NEW YORK

NEW JERSEY

TEXAS FLORIDA

Distribution

- California: 13,232, or 19%
- Florida: 11,248, or 16%
- New Jersey: 11,175, or 16%
- New York: 7,845, or 11%
- Texas: 3,302, or 5%

Useful websites

Costa Rica (www.ramsar.org/wurchbk3cs3.doc)
Costa Rica History
  (http://incostarica.net/docs/history)

Festivals

Catholic holidays such as "Semana Santa" (Easter Week).
Independence Day (September 15).

Jobs

Finance and business.

Religion

Roman Catholicism.

Language

Spanish.

Region of origin

Costa Rica, Central America.

Population

2000 U.S. census:
est. 69,000

Food

Meat tamales, *ensalada Rusa* (Russian salad).

Quiltmaking

The Amish women of Pennsylvania and Ohio are famous for their skill in quiltmaking. The Hmong women of Vietnam are also accomplished needlewomen, making beautiful appliqué and embroidered work called *pa ndao*. Some Hmong immigrants to the United States have begun working with Amish women to create quilts combining the best of both traditions. Their collaboration shows how artists from different cultures can find a common interest and language in a shared craft, and how crafts continue to evolve as long as there are people to practice them.

Crafts can be defined as the traditional knowledge of a group, especially the knowledge of how to make the things needed for everyday life. Before the Industrial Revolution of the 19th century, when technology began to replace older manufacturing techniques, nearly everything was made by hand, from houses to horseshoes and waterpumps to weathervanes, by someone skilled in that craft.

When the first European immigrants came to the American continent, they had to leave behind almost everything they owned and make a new life in a new country. What they could bring with them was their knowledge, and they used that knowledge to create everything they needed. Blacksmiths, who work in metal, made horseshoes and door hinges. Carpenters were busy building houses, furniture, and wagons out of wood. Weavers wove the cloth that seamstresses sewed into clothing and quilts. Stonemasons built stone walls and carved headstones for the graveyard. Farmers used their traditional knowledge of plants, weather, and growing seasons to produce food to keep the settlers alive.

Traditional Crafts

Each group that came to America's shores brought with them unique knowledge and ways of doing things that were traditional in their home culture. So, for example, English settlers built their houses with thatched roofs made of dried grasses and walls of half-wood, half-plaster, similar to the ones they knew at home. Their German neighbors, however, crafted their homes out of whole logs, relying on the knowledge they had learned in Germany. Mexican crafts such as cooking with spicy chilis and building with adobe are still common in the American Southwest, where many Mexican immigrants settled. Africans had an enormous impact on the crafts of the Deep South, meanwhile, affecting everything from farming techniques to food preparation. One example is the coiled sweetgrass baskets that are made today by the Gullah people of South Carolina, a continuation of a craft that was brought to America from West Africa more than 300 years ago.

Native Americans also contributed to the creation of American crafts by sharing their traditional knowledge with new settlers. The earliest European immigrants to American shores relied on the experience and learning of local Native American peoples to identify foods that were safe to eat and how to cook them, hunting techniques for new types of animals, and ways of using plants that Europeans had never seen before. From Native Americans European immigrants learned how to grow corn, to cook turkey, to build canoes, and to cure scurvy with pine bark. In turn the Native American

A Gullah boy in South Carolina sells coiled sweetgrass baskets that his mother has made. Slaves brought the craft from West Africa over 300 years ago.

peoples adopted some of the materials and knowledge of the immigrants. The Navajo people of the western United States were already accomplished weavers when the Spaniards first arrived in their country. However, the beautiful Navajo rugs and blankets woven today would not be the same without the wool that became available after the introduction of European sheep.

New American Crafts

As the American nation developed American crafts developed too. Traditional knowledge was passed on from master to apprentice. Knowledge was also passed along in families, usually from father to son or mother to daughter, since some crafts were considered "women's work" (such as sewing, quilting, needlework, cooking, and preserving food) and others "men's work" (carpentry, blacksmithing, fishing, and farming). As various groups began to share their knowledge and develop new ways of living in a new land, new "American" crafts emerged, such as the colorful quilts of the Amish or the fine furniture of the Shaker religious colony.

It was not until the early 20th century that machine-made items became available and affordable for most Americans, and only then did people's dependence on the skill to craft everyday items disappear. While it is true that most people do not need to make the necessities of life anymore, American crafts have not disappeared. Many are now hobbies, and people still enjoy quilting, woodcarving, or pottery, even though they do not really need the items they are making. In addition, new crafts are being added to American culture, as descendants of immigrants relearn traditional skills, and continuing immigration brings new crafts to the United States.

Stonecarving

Two Italian American stonecarvers have overseen the creation of stone carvings in and on the National Cathedral in Washington, D.C. Trained in the stonecutting studios of Italy, both Roger Morigi and Vincent Palumbo eventually emigrated to the United States and used their skills to create beautiful statues, decorations, columns, and walls for America's National Cathedral. The combination of traditional skill with modern ideas can be seen in the whimsical and monstrous gargoyles that sit high on the cathedral's roof. Traditionally found on medieval churches, gargoyles are waterspouts carved to look like monsters. The National Cathedral has some gargoyles that refer to the monsters of the 20th century, including a computer, a camera, and even one that has the face of Darth Vader from *Star Wars*.

See also

- Amish (Volume 1)
- Architecture (Volume 1)
- Navajo (Volume 8)
- Trades and professions (Volume 10)

Numerous stereotypes have linked immigrants with crime, from Irish heavies, Russian anarchists, and Italian mobsters in the past to black gangs today. Despite such images, immigrants are no more prone to criminal activity than any other group of people. Indeed, many immigrant groups form strong internal bonds, often through community organizations that help maintain standards of behavior. As in society as a whole, however, immigrants who feel marginalized, who are economically or socially disadvantaged, or who suffer prejudice may gravitate toward crime.

Organized Crime

Ethnic-based forms of crime can take multiple forms affecting both society at large and the particular community in which they take place. Ethnic crime often takes on some type of organizational form. These organizations can range from those involved in specific hate crimes, such as the Ku Klux Klan, through to the localized violence of street gangs, like the Bloods and Crips, and on to complex forms of organized crime, such as the Chinese "tongs" and the Italian "Mafia."

Tongs were particularly active in U.S. cities from the 1850s to 1920s. Originally they grew out of the Chinese community's desire to protect itself from marginalization. Tongs were based on benevolent political–religious associations in China and were founded by Chinese immigrants to America to deal with lawless members of their own community as well as discrimination from white American society. While some retained these functions, others became involved in criminal activities, such as the opium trade, gambling, and selling protection. Different tongs often became involved in disputes and gang wars. Criminal tongs began to disappear as the Chinese population became less marginalized. Some social historians believe the same is now true of the Mafia.

Many popular cultural phenomena, such as Mario Puzo's award-winning "Godfather" novels (and the movie series of the same name), have gone into great depth about the humble and somewhat altruistic beginnings of the Italian American Mafia. Many historians agree that the Italian American Mafia served

Alphonse ("Al") Capone (1899–1948) came to symbolize all that was ruthless and violent in America in the 1920s. Born the son of Italian immigrants, Capone went on to establish himself as the most powerful Mafia boss in Chicago during the era of prohibition. He was eventually jailed for tax evasion.

largely as a system of protection with its own set of rules and regulations. The Mafia supposedly did serve as a form of social justice in neighborhoods that were considered beneath official notice, populated by people who were looked on as outcasts. Some Italian immigrants faced with such a situation turned to a traditional source of social stability borrowed from their "old country"—the Mafia. Feared and respected Mafia figures emerged from the very streets they were "policing." However, under the guise of helping their local communities, many mafia members made vast profits from the vices and weaknesses of those under their so-called "protection."

Street Gangs

Another prime example of the dual nature of ethnic crime is the youth gang. Youths, both male and female, have historically banded together within different organizations, ranging from social cliques to street gangs, in an effort to establish support structures. They flock toward people whom they identify as similar to themselves—often members of the same ethnic or racial group. These groups then seek to outline their sphere of influence as *their* territory, *their* neighborhood. They lay claim to *their* community and protect these abstract boundaries—sometimes by setting up an underground economy, like the drug trade, and other times by violence.

The intergang ethnic rivalries portrayed in such classic films as Leonard Bernstein's *West Side Story* were a reality in the 1950s. Yet the ethnically and racially homogeneous gang wars of the late 20th century, embodied in the high rates of black-on-black drug-related violence, reveal that the urban tradition of interethnic rivalry is no act of hatred and ignorance but rather an articulation of economic, social, political, and cultural competition. However, the larger umbrella gang organizations, like the Bloods and the Crips, have made millions of dollars and gained social status from fear because such gangs are able to flourish through drugs and violence. It is only by striking fear into their own communities that they are able to escape the reach of law enforcement agencies.

Recent surveys have identified an increase in criminal gangs among the Native American communities in the United States and Canada, including the so-called "Warrior gangs," the Ruthless Deuce, and Native Gangster Bloods. Their growth also appears to be linked to marginalization and deprivation. Many gang members come from dysfunctional families and have lost contact with their traditional cultures. Some tribes are beginning to set up gang intervention units and task forces to address the problem. Such community initiatives are often effective in turning people away from crime. Organizations like church groups, kinship groups, and youth centers cultivate a sense of togetherness and belonging in a positive environment.

Bloods and Crips

The Los Angeles-based Bloods and Crips are probably the two most widely known street gangs in the United States due to the extensive media exposure they received in the 1980s. These groups have migrated throughout North America, and members are found in most states and their prison populations. There are now hundreds of gangs under the main Blood and Crip names. Originally made up of black members only, these gangs are no longer racially specific.

See also

- Ghettos (Volume 4)
- Hispanic Americans (Volume 5)
- Italians (Volume 6)
- Nativism (Volume 8)
- Urban reform and race (Volume 10)

Croatians

Croatians, like other immigrants to the United States, came to pursue their dreams in a new land. Large-scale immigration began at the end of the 19th century, and Croatians have since assimilated into North American culture and established themselves in all parts of society. Homeland politics, however, have remained an important focal point for the Croatian population abroad. Today every third Croatian lives outside of Croatia. In the United States they have settled around the large industrial centers of the Northeast, but there are significant communities in the Midwest as well.

Waves of Immigration

Mass emigration of Croatians to North America began in the 1880s, but Croatian records date their arrival in America to 1526 and in Canada to 1543. Some historians maintain that Croatians took part in Christopher Columbus's historic voyage in 1492. Croatia established diplomatic ties with the United States in 1783, when it sent a diplomat to ask if American harbors would be open for Croatian ships. The Americans agreed. These earliest Croatians in North America were mainly soldiers of fortune trying to earn money in the New World to send to their families. They roamed in search of opportunities rather than settling into communities.

The first true Croatian settlers in North America were peasants from the Austro-Hungarian Empire, which then controlled Croatia. They migrated when the empire went to war with Turkey in the 1870s. In Canada they settled mainly in Ontario. The first Croatian colonies in the United States were founded in the 1880s on the Mississippi Delta in Louisiana and in California.

The next wave of Croatian immigrants found employment in the mills and mines of large industrial centers like Pittsburgh, Chicago, and Detroit. They worked in iron foundries, steel mills, factories, railyards, and coal mines. Pittsburgh became home to the largest concentration of Croatians between 1880 and 1914. By 1901 more than 13,000 Croats lived in the area.

The third wave of immigrants arrived after World War II and were generally better educated and more urbanized than the previous groups. They reinforced social and political groups, and began new educational, cultural, and religious organizations, which laid the roots for today's strong Croatian community in North America.

Croatian Communities and Culture

Over the past 150 years Croatians have founded numerous political, fraternal, and cultural organizations. One of the first was the Croatian

Many post-World War II Croatian immigrants were employed as factory workers and operators of machinery, such as in this steel-milling plant in Pittsburgh, Pennsylvania, 1954.

Distribution

Most populous states:
- Pennsylvania
- Indiana
- Ohio
- New Jersey
- New York
- Michigan (Upper Peninsula)
- Minnesota

Most populous cities:
- Pittsburgh, Pennsylvania
- Gary, Indiana

MINNESOTA MICHIGAN OHIO NEW YORK

INDIANA NEW JERSEY

PENNSYLVANIA

Region of origin

Croatia

The Balkans region of southeast Europe.

Population

258,733 in United States (2000 census).

First immigrants

Possibly came with Christopher Columbus, 1492.

Food

Burek (a layered pie made of meat or cheese), *piroska* (a cheese donut), *struckle* (cottage cheese rolls), and *manistra od bobica* (beans and fresh corn soup).

Religion

Predominantly Roman Catholic.

Language

Croatian and English.

Community organizations

The Croatian Fraternal Union (CFU).

The CFU provides insurance and financial planning for its members. Its lodges across the United States and Canada also support sporting events, cultural and social programs, and scholarships.

The Croatian American Cultural Center in Sacramento, California (www.cacc.com/)

Croatian American Association (http://public.srce.hr/~mprofaca/caa.html)

Croatian American Society (www.cas.hr/)

Croatian Genealogical Society (http://feefhs.org/cro/frg-cghs.html)

Canadian Croatian Congress (www.crocc.org/)

Dates of major arrivals

- 1880–1914: A major wave of immigrant workers settled in Pittsburgh, Chicago, and Detroit, and took work in the heavy industries of the northeastern United States. By 1901, 13,000 had settled in Pittsburgh, Pennsylvania.

Jobs

The earliest Croatian immigrants worked as fishermen and fruit growers. At the end of the 19th century men worked in iron and steel plants, factories, and railyards, and as coal miners.

Festivals

New Year's Day: January 1 (Nova Godina).

Eastern Orthodox Christmas: January 6–7 (2002) (Pravoslavni Botic).

Easter: April (Uskrs).

May Day: May 1 (Praznik Rada).

Day of Croatia: May 30 (Independence Day or Dan Drtavnosti).

Day of Insurrection: June 22 (World War II) (Dan Ustanka).

Thanksgiving Day: August 5 (Liberation Day, 1999) (Dan Domovinske Zahvalnosti).

Feast of the Assumption: August (Velika Gospa).

All Saints' Day: November 1 (Day of Death) (Dan Mrtvih).

Christmas Eve: December 24 (Roman Catholic) (Badnjak).

Christmas Day: December 25 (Roman Catholic) (Botia Katolicki).

A group of Croatian dancers performing at Expo 86, Vancouver, British Columbia, Canada.

Nikola Tesla

One of the most prominent Croatians was scientist and inventor Nikola Tesla (1856–1943). He worked for Thomas Edison in Orange, New Jersey, and later established the Tesla Laboratory and Tesla Electric Company. His patents led to the invention of radio.

See also

- Albanians (Volume 1)
- Bosnians (Volume 1)
- Serbians (Volume 9)

Workers' Benefit Society. The organization was set up to protect Croatian workers in the Pittsburgh steel industry's low-paying, high-risk jobs. Originally intended to insure their medical expenses and funeral costs, the organization's branches flourished. Eventually many merged to form the Croatian Fraternal Union.

Numerous Croatian Catholic parishes also sprang up, not only helping to maintain Croatian faith, language, and solidarity, but also assisting immigrants to adapt to their new country. As the number of permanent Croatian immigrants increased, the need for education for their children also grew. The schools were, and remain, mainly under the auspices of the local parish.

An important aspect of all Croatian communities in North America has been the preservation of various forms of folk culture, including arts, crafts, folk art, dances, music, games, stories, and musical instruments. Croatians have been particularly active in the art scene in North America, including literature, theater, and fine arts. In art sculptor Ivan Mestrovic (1883–1962) became the first living artist in the history of the Metropolitan Museum of Art in New York to be honored with a one-man show. In sports Croatians have also competed successfully, particularly in Canadian club soccer.

Croatian newspapers have also played an important role in preserving Croatian national identity in North America. About 250 newspapers, periodicals, almanacs, and magazines have emerged since the first publication appeared in 1884—it was *Slavenska Sloga* (Slavic Unity), which was founded in that year in San Francisco.

Croatian Politics

The violent suppression of the so-called "Croatian Spring"—a liberalization movement that took place in Croatia in 1971—created a new generation of exiles. The Croatian Spring was a student-led movement brutally quashed by order of Yugoslavian communist leader Marshal Tito. However, Croatian nationalism continued to increase, and in 1990 the Croatian Democratic Union came to power. In 1991 Croatia broke away from Yugoslavia to become independent. However, the ethnic and national unrest that have plagued the Balkans continued. Armed clashes spread through Serb enclaves in Croatia, and the Yugoslav army invaded. Although it withdrew under United Nations auspices, tensions remained, and the Croatian government only took full control of its territories from Serbia in 1998.

Croatian Americans have been torn between regard for their homeland and involvement in U.S. politics. Croatian organizations have long lobbied for political goals abroad and in the 1990s raised money to aid independent Croatia.

During colonial times (1607–1776) disputes to determine the United States–Canada border led to several wars between the British and the French. The British colonies, referred to as "New England," extended north to the St. Lawrence River and east to include the present-day regions of Acadia and Nova Scotia. The French territory of "New France" included lands north and west of the St. Lawrence River, including the island of Newfoundland. The first major conflict was King William's War (1689–1690), which included several massacres and raids by both French and English forces across the St. Lawrence River. Other conflicts ensued. Competing land claims, in which both Britain and France claimed ownership, were common in this period and made determining the actual border difficult. In addition, the native population and French and English fur traders moved extensively between the disputed territories with little concern for political or legal boundaries.

The continued efforts of the British to rid the Americas of the French were finally successful during the French and Indian War (1754–1763). General James Wolfe defeated the French forces at the Battle of Quebec in September 1759, and Montreal fell to the British soon afterward. In the peace treaty that followed the war the French renounced all claims to their American, Indian, and Caribbean territories. The unification of the American and Canadian colonies under British rule meant that for a time, it was no longer necessary to attempt to define a border between the American colonies.

The War of Independence

During the American Revolution (1775–1783) the Canadians allied with the British against the American colonies. After the American colonies achieved independence, the location of the northern border again became an issue. The treaty ending the War of Independence declared the territory north of the United States to be simply "Canada," although no specific border was determined at that time. The Louisiana Purchase in 1803—which saw the United States acquire 800,000 square miles (1.28 million sq. km) of French territory—extended the western boundary of the United States to the Rocky Mountains and made the establishment of a northern boundary vital. Some of the fighting in the war between the United States and Britain in 1812–1815 took place on Canadian soil. American forces attacked Canada five times, but on each occasion they were repulsed, showing Canada's determination to remain separate.

In 1818 a convention with Britain established the northern border of the Louisiana Purchase territory at 49° north latitude. Maine became a state in 1820, but it

General James Wolfe of the British Army and Field Marshall Louis-Joseph de Montcalm, the commander of the French forces, depicted during the Battle of Quebec in 1759. Both men were mortally wounded on the battlefield, but the British victory was decisive in driving the French out of North America.

The northernmost point of the Alaska–Canada border on the Arctic coast. In this photograph, taken in 1924, engineers of the U.S. Coast and Geodetic Survey display American and British flags to delineate the frontier.

Alaska and Illegal Immigration

Under Operation Cheechako in October 1997 U.S. government agents apprehended 55 unauthorized workers employed in the Bering Sea fishing industry in Alaska, 35 of whom were Mexican. Immigration and Naturalization Service officers arrested a further 20 unauthorized workers in February 2000, again in the fishing industry. Most of the workers were again Mexicans. The agents said they had inspected 30 fishing boats and found illegal workers on 10 of them. Jobs in the fishing industry pay well, often require minimal skills, and demand only physical labor, so migrant workers are attracted to them. Also, Mexicans do not require a visa in order to enter Canada, making getting to Alaska relatively straightforward. In addition, in contrast to the continental United States, Alaskan industries are less likely to be checked for illegal workers.

was 1842 before a treaty established the Maine–Canada border of today. The addition of the Oregon Territory brought the western border of the United States to the Pacific Ocean. The Treaty of Oregon in 1846 made 49° north latitude the official border with Canada, where it remains today.

In 1867 the United States purchased Alaska from Russia, thus completing the American territory that borders Canada today. Russia and Canada had established the Alaskan border in 1825, so there was no border dispute between America and Canada after the purchase. The last area of the border to be clarified was the boundary through the Lake of the Woods in Minnesota. A treaty between Britain and the United States established this part of the border in 1925, completing the frontier that exists today.

Canadian Border Control

The border between the continental United States and Canada stretches approximately 4,000 miles (6,400 km), spanning vast expanses of woods, pasture lands, and lakes. The border between Canada and Alaska adds another 1,500 miles (2,400 km) for the Border Patrol and the Immigration and Naturalization Service to police. Today there are only 291 agents assigned to the northern U.S. border. More than 250,000 people arrive daily from Canada by official ports of entry. In 1999 there were over 200 million two-way border crossings.

Border Patrol agents maintain 132 legal ports of entry along the frontier, including 3 in Alaska, 12 in Washington, 2 in Idaho, 11 in Montana, 18 in North Dakota, 4 in Michigan, 7 in Minnesota, 7 in New York, 5 in Vermont, and 10 in Maine. Nearly 75 percent of all crossings between the United States and Canada occur at only four ports of entry: Blaine, Washington; Port Huron, Michigan; Detroit, Michigan; and Buffalo, New York. Since 1924 the Border Patrol's primary mission has been to detect and prevent the illegal entry of aliens into the United States, as well as to facilitate the flow of legal immigration and goods. However, today, another main objective has become the detection and prevention of any potential terrorist activity.

Techniques of the Border Patrol

To accomplish its mission, the Border Patrol maintains surveillance, responds to electronic sensor alarms and aircraft sightings, and interprets and follows tracks. "Signcutting" involves interpreting any disturbances in natural terrain conditions that might indicate the passage of people, animals, or vehicles. Transportation checks involve regular inspections of buses, commercial aircraft, passenger and freight trains, and marine craft. Air operations also play a role, with planes and helicopters providing important information on movements on the ground. In an effort to curtail illegal immigration and smuggling over water, the Border Patrol maintains 55 vessels in 16 sectors. These boats are particularly valuable along the waterways that separate the United States and Canada, including the Inside Passage (Alaska), the Straits of Juan de Fuca and the Puget Sound (Washington), the Great Lakes, and the St. Lawrence River. The United States Coast Guard and Coast Guard Auxiliary often provide support for the Border Patrol in these areas.

In 1988 the U.S.–Canadian Bilateral Consultative Group was established to work closely on issues affecting both countries. The group met in 2000 to plan ways to work together to coordinate immigration policies, improve cooperation between law enforcement agencies, counter terrorism, and share intelligence information. In 2001 President George W. Bush stated that he envisioned a U.S. border that provided a strong barrier against all external threats, while posing little or no obstacle to legitimate trade and travel. The tragic events of September 11, 2001, highlighted the need for the strengthening of border defenses. In an effort to achieve this, 20 Border Patrol agents were added to the port of entry at Blaine, Washington, 12 were added in Spokane, Washington, and 32 new video cameras were installed to monitor remote locations east of Blaine.

The Smart Border Declaration

On December 12, 2001, Tom Ridge, director of the U.S. Office of Homeland Security, and John Manley, then Canada's minister of foreign affairs, signed the Smart Border Declaration. It is a 30-point action plan to help speed up and secure the flow of goods between the United States and Canada. The plan is to develop a "secure card" for permanent residents, review screening of refugee claimants, develop an automated immigration database to share customs data, and create an integrated approach to processing truck, rail, and marine cargo away from border areas.

An officer of the U.S. Border Patrol checks a vehicle at a roadblock. The Border Patrol was established on May 28, 1924, and its primary mission remains the same today: to detect and prevent the illegal entry of aliens and contraband into the United States.

Peace Arch State Park

This 20-acre park in Blaine, Washington, commemorates the signing of the Treaty of Ghent (1814), which ended the War of 1812 between Britain and the United States, and the Rush-Bagot Agreement (1818) that ended the prospect of the militarization of the Great Lakes. The 67-foot (20m) Peace Arch is jointly maintained by the United States and Canada to celebrate the nonmilitarized border. The arch was begun in 1920.

See also

• Cross-border migration, Mexican (Volume 3)
• Illegal immigration (Volume 5)
• Immigration legislation, U.S. (Volume 5)

Legal Activities

According to the Bureau of Transportation Services, in 1997 approximately 300 Border Patrol officers stationed on the Canadian border processed 5,768,071 trucks crossing north to south, as well as 30,337 trains. A total of 520,268 pedestrians crossed the border on foot, in addition to 37,362,998 personal vehicles containing 90,731,418 passengers. These numbers provide some indication of the scale of the task assigned to the northern Border Patrol.

Illegal Activities

Along the northern border of the United States most illegal immigration has been attempted at official ports of entry using false claims of United States citizenship, misrepresented purposes of entry, as well as fraudulent or improper documentation. Some people try to enter without inspection between ports of entry. For example, the Swanton, Vermont, port of entry recently broke a smuggling ring that brought illegal Asian immigrants into the United States by way of Native American tribal lands that straddled the border. In all, 16,344 illegal aliens were seized along the Canadian border in 1997.

Today, the Border Patrol faces two serious challenges: drug smuggling and terrorism. Cross-border drug smuggling activities appear to be centered in British Columbia, Canada, an area with a long history of marijuana trafficking into the United States. Between 1995 and 1997 the amount of marijuana crossing the border more than quadrupled, with confiscations increasing 87 percent between 1996 and 1997 alone. In spite of increased efforts to halt this smuggling, officials estimate that, at best, only 10 percent of the drugs are confiscated.

The second serious threat is the infiltration of suspected terrorists into the United States via unmonitored sections of the northern border. The terrorists involved in the World Trade Center bombing entered the country apparently using Canadian immigration papers. It is also believed that some of them entered the United States by way of the Canadian border.

The development of a more effective border management system is ongoing. The United States and Canada want to expand trade connections while preventing terrorist infiltration, illegal immigration, and drug smuggling. A U.S. government budget proposal included $11 billion for border security; the Canadian government proposed $5 billion. The aim was to create an air, land, and sea border that offered better protection yet did not impede the flow of legal trade.

According to the U.S. Department of Transportation, 290 million people entered the United States across the Mexican border in 2001. This number does not include illegal immigrants, whose numbers can only be guessed. The U.S. Border Patrol estimates it catches one alien in five; other observers suggest the agency catches only one in ten. In 2000 the U.S. Border Patrol apprehended 1,643,679 people illegally trying to enter the country. Of those caught, 97 percent returned voluntarily to Mexico; many to try to cross the border again later. The Border Patrol also reports an increase in illegal immigrants from Central and South America, East Asia, and the Middle East. The illegal trafficking of humans and drugs across the border is recognized as a serious problem by the U.S. government. Due to the historically high rate of immigration and trafficking, controls and policing of the U.S.–Mexico border are more intensive than of the U.S.–Canada border.

Illegal Immigrants from Countries Other than Mexico

Immigrants of other nationalities have a history of crossing into the United States using the Mexican border. In 1907 Marcus Braun, the newly appointed inspector-at-large of the Immigration Bureau, traveled to Mexico to investigate illegal immigration. He discovered migrants from Syria, Greece, Japan, and China immigrating to Mexico, obtaining false documentation, then being smuggled into the United States. A large number of Japanese, Turkish, Syrian, Guatemalan, Korean, and European immigrants entered Laredo, Texas, between 1903 and 1907. During the same period Japanese, Palestinians, Syrians, Canadians, and Filipinos entered through Brownsville, Texas, according to the Immigration Bureau.

Today this multinational immigration continues. The Border Patrol refers to illegal immigrants from other countries as "OTMs" (Other Than Mexicans). In 2000 U.S. officials caught 28,598 OTMs crossing the Mexican border, of whom more than 22,000 were from Honduras, El Salvador, and Guatemala. These immigrants create special problems because they cannot be shipped back to Mexico; they must be flown home. Despite a steady trickle of OTMs, 99.9 percent of the illegal immigrants apprehended on the southwest border in 2001 were from Mexico and 16 other Latin American countries.

The Texas Rangers

Established on August 10, 1823, the Texas Rangers are the oldest law enforcement body in North America with statewide jurisdiction. They were originally formed to protect settlers against hostile Indians and Mexican bandits. When the U.S. war with Mexico ended in 1848, Texas became first an independent republic, then a state. United States Army troops protected the border with Mexico until Texas seceded from the Union in 1861, leaving the job once again to the Texas Rangers. In 1865 the triumphant Union military authorities disbanded the Ranger force. By the end of the 1870s, however, the continued threat of Indians and pillaging by Mexican bandits along the Rio Grande brought the Texas Rangers back. Along with the Border Patrol they continue to help protect the border areas across Texas to this day. The photograph shows three armed Texas Rangers patrolling a border area on horseback in 1915.

History of Border Control

The United States began passing laws to limit immigration in 1875. Convicts, "immoral women," idiots, lunatics, and "persons who might become [a] public charge" were excluded. In 1882 the first Chinese exclusion law was passed, which created a Chinese Immigration Service to control entry into the United States. Many people began entering the country illegally, and the U.S. government created a Bureau of Immigration in 1885 to stop them. It was well known that illegal Chinese immigrants disembarked on the Mexican west coast, walked overland to central Mexico, and tried to cross at the border town of Juarez, Chihuahua. From there they were smuggled into El Paso and on to other parts of the United States.

Border Laws

In 1891 the treasury secretary decided to "prescribe rules for inspection along the borders of Canada, British Columbia, and Mexico so as not to obstruct or unnecessarily delay, impede, or annoy passengers in ordinary travel between said countries." By 1899 there were four Chinese Immigrant Service inspectors along the Mexican border: in Nogales, Arizona, El Paso, Texas, Laredo, Texas, and Piedras Negras, Mexico. By 1901 inspectors were also stationed in Tucson, Arizona, and San Diego, California. Officers on the border during these early years mainly concentrated on enforcing the Chinese exclusion laws. After the passage of the Immigration Act of 1907 the

A customs inspector at the border crossing at Nogales, Arizona, interviews a driver as he enters the United States from Mexico.

Mexican migrant workers ready to start work on farms in the San Joaquin River delta as part of the Bracero program in 1942.

individual border stations were reorganized into the Mexican Border District, containing California, Arizona, New Mexico, and Texas—a borderline stretching approximately 1,951 miles (3,200km).

There were almost no restrictions against Mexicans until the U.S. Immigration Act of 1917. This act required immigrants to pay a head tax of eight dollars to immigrate into the United States, and they also had to pass a literacy test. Illegal immigration flourished until the early years of the 20th century, when it was disrupted by restrictions brought about by the Mexican Revolution and World War I. After this period prohibited crossings accelerated again.

The U.S. Border Patrol, as part of the Immigration Bureau, was established on May 28, 1924. Started in El Paso, it employed 450 officers. Its main duties were to prevent smuggling and arrest illegal entrants. Most illegal immigrants from Mexico came only to visit their families or to work briefly in border towns. During Prohibition (1919–1933) smuggling absorbed most of the attention of the Border Patrol. Whiskey bootleggers avoided the bridges and slipped their forbidden cargo across the Rio Grande River by way of pack mules.

Border Patrol Today

By the end of World War II Border Patrol employees numbered 8,000. During the war the force provided tighter control of the border, manned alien detention camps, guarded diplomats, and assisted the Coast Guard in searching for enemy saboteurs. For the first time the border was patrolled by air. The McCarran–Walter Act of 1952 established the immigration laws in effect today. That same year Border Patrol officers were first permitted to search for illegal immigrants anywhere in the United States. Illegal entrants traveling

Bracero Program

During World War II a serious labor shortage developed in the United States when many men left to fight in the war. Farmers needed help, so the Border Patrol recruited Mexican nationals. On August 4, 1942, the United States and Mexico signed the Mexican Farm Labor Program Agreement, the first agreement aimed at legalizing and controlling Mexican migrant farm workers. The agreement guaranteed a minimum wage of 30 cents an hour and humane treatment in the form of adequate shelter, food, and sanitation for the workers. Between 1942 and 1964 more than 4.5 million *braceros* (Spanish for "manual laborer") entered the United States. It has been estimated that in the 1950s the United States imported as many as 300,000 Mexican workers annually. However, the program had serious side effects. Illegal immigration soared as those not chosen as *braceros* sought to enter the country anyway. Furthermore, with the phasing out of the program many former *braceros* simply turned around in Mexico and crossed illegally back into the United States.

within the country were for the first time subject to arrest. The early 1960s saw the beginning of drug smuggling across the border. The Border Patrol now assists other agencies in intercepting these drugs.

U.S. Intelligence reports and actual experience indicate that the smuggling of drugs and of illegal immigrants are often linked. Illegal immigrants seeking assistance from alien smugglers—sometimes called "coyotes"—are often forced to carry drugs into the United States in part payment for their passage. Some Mexican police and immigration officials are also involved in this highly lucrative trade.

Activities such as commerce, visiting, and legal migration form a vital part of the migration across the Mexican border. Many thousands of people legally cross the border daily, mainly transporting merchandise to and from the United States. In addition, visitors, businessmen, entertainers, and others enter the United States to see family, attend conferences, conduct business, and give concerts. Immigration officials along the U.S.–Mexican border processed 290 million entrants in 2001.

Customs special agents use all-terrain vehicles and are specially trained in tracking cross-border movements of people, goods, and money.

Leaving for the United States

Most people in Latin America leave their country because of a failing economy, a catastrophe, political instability, or personal reasons. The trip north to the U.S.–Mexican border is arduous; untold numbers of illegals each year are attacked, robbed, raped, murdered, or enslaved by immigrant smugglers. If they make it across Mexico and past the Mexican and American border patrols, they still need to get to a city, find a job, and locate a place to live. Some are arrested and sent home, while others end up in gangs or are used by the unscrupulous as low-paid "slave labor." If they are very lucky, some will be able to become citizens and bring other family members to the United States to live. The dangerous journey is often undertaken only by those who are truly desperate, for whom it provides hope—of a job, a home, and a better future. Even if they are arrested and sent home, these illegals may have been able to work for a while and send money to their families. If they remain undetected, any children born in the United States will be able to claim citizenship. For many who have had their lives devastated by hurricanes, storms, floods, earthquakes, volcanic eruptions, revolutions, civil war, economic depression, and political instability, the United States seems blessedly peaceful.

Economic and Political Migration

In addition to the natural disasters suffered by Central America, many countries, including Mexico, have experienced severe economic crises, leading to unemployment and poverty. Mexico, for example, has one of the largest oil reserves in the world. In the 1970s the price of oil rose. Investors from the United States and Europe invested heavily. Mexico overborrowed and overspent. When oil prices plunged, Mexico could not repay the loans. As a result, the peso collapsed, inflation ran wild, and the economy suffered. Immigration to the United States rose precipitously soon afterward.

Political instability, revolutions, and civil wars have plagued Central America for decades. A variety of wars have raged in Guatemala for the past 30 years. The civil war in El Salvador lasted from 1980 to 1992. Nicaragua experienced civil war from 1976 to 1990. Dictatorships in Cuba, Chile, and Haiti have also led people to flee, some through Mexico and into the United States. Neighboring countries like Honduras and the Dominican Republic have also been weakened by the region's political and economic instability.

Immigrant workers

In addition to the factors that drive people to leave their country there are elements that motivate people to come specifically to the United States. Between 1942 and 1964 the U.S. government actively encouraged the entry of Mexican farm laborers in the Bracero Program (see box on page 23). Today the H2A Guestworker Program is a similar plan that addresses labor shortages in agriculture. H2A workers come from Mexico and all over Latin America and the Caribbean.

The demand for cheap labor in the United States also attracts illegal immigrants. In 2000, 50 percent of the U.S. agricultural labor force was undocumented—about 1.5 million workers, most of whom were from Mexico. Undocumented migrants also work in meat packing, food processing, hotels and restaurants, manufacturing and cleaning, as well as virtually all other low-wage sectors. U.S. employers value immigrant labor—regardless of legal status—because migrant laborers work hard, complain little (illegal immigrants have no legal rights), and take jobs others will not accept.

Immigrants also come to the United States for personal reasons: to be reunited with loved ones, friends, or family—especially spouses. Of the legal immigrants admitted in 1997, 67.1 percent were family-sponsored, and more than half were the spouses of American citizens.

Operation Wetback

"Operation Wetback" was a U.S. government operation to coerce illegal Mexican agricultural workers (called *mojados*, or "wetbacks") back to Mexico using quasi-military force. In Texas on July 15, 1954, the Immigration and Naturalization Service (INS) apprehended 4,800 illegal immigrants. After the first day the daily arrests averaged about 1,100. A major concern of the operation was to discourage reentry by moving the workers far into the interior of Mexico. The U.S. government used no more than 700 men; but Border Patrol officials, who hoped to scare illegal workers to flee into Mexico, exaggerated the numbers involved. The operation trailed off in the fall of 1954 as INS funding began to run out. The INS estimates that as many as 1.3 million illegal immigrants were forced to leave by the operation; however, many commentators considered this figure to be exaggerated. Official estimates in Texas were slightly more than 80,000.

Specialized truckstops, such as the Otay Mesa crossing, facilitate trade between Mexico and the United States, and allow for immigration checks to be made.

Anti-immigrant feeling

Resentment of immigrants—both legal and illegal—is often felt by communities with significant immigrant populations. Immigrants are sometimes viewed as a drain on social services and a threat to the existing workforce. In California, which attracts the highest number of illegal immigrants from Mexico and Latin America, there was a severe backlash of feeling against these immigrants in the 1990s. In 1994 a majority of the state's voters approved Proposition 187, although it was later outlawed by the state's supreme court. The proposition aimed to prevent illegal immigrants from receiving education, health care, and other social services.

See also

- Hispanic Americans (Volume 5)
- Illegal immigration (Volume 5)
- Immigration and Naturalization Service (Volume 5)
- Mexican immigration/emigration (Volume 7)
- Mexicans (Volume 7)

Both the United States and Mexico have become increasingly concerned in recent years about the number of injuries and fatalities in the border area. On June 19, 1998, both countries announced an agreement to increase efforts to save migrant lives.

Each year the Mexican and American border patrols save thousands of people abandoned by unscrupulous smugglers in mountains, deserts, and rivers. The Binational Border Safety Initiative targets prevention, search and rescue, identification, and the tracking and recording of immigrants. The United States is working closely with Mexican consulates to discourage illegal crossings and educate people about the dangers of trusting smugglers. Each year "Cold/Hot Weather" campaigns are used to warn people about the dangers of heat, cold, swollen rivers, mountains, and deserts through public service announcements on TV, radio, and fliers. The initiative also prosecutes those who smuggle people across the border. In 1999 Border Patrol rescue efforts saved 1,042 people in 200 incidents. This program realized a 21 percent decrease in drowning deaths and a 41 percent decrease in heat-related deaths between 1998 and 1999.

Current concerns

Cross-border migration, legal and illegal, as well as the smuggling of drugs and people remain key issues of concern for both the United States and Mexican governments. Discussions between the two countries to grant amnesty to some illegal Mexican immigrants already in the United States in return for Mexico tightening up its southern border controls to stem the flow of immigrants and address drug trafficking issues were halted after September 11, 2001. The terrorist attacks in New York and Washington heightened U.S. concerns about security. Tentative talks resumed in May 2002.

Cubans

Cuban Americans are one of the highest-profile ethnic minority groups currently living in the United States. They have arrived in substantial numbers since the Cuban Revolution of 1959, when Fidel Castro overthrew the dictator Fulgencio Batista and turned Cuba into a Marxist state.

Patterns of Migration

Some Cubans migrated to the United States in the 19th century. A number of early migrants were cigar merchants who left during the period of 1868 to 1878 and settled in Florida. This wave of emigration was caused by the Ten Years' War, a struggle for Cuban independence from Spain. Another wave came during the last years of the Batista regime in the late 1950s, when 10,000 to 15,000 Cubans—mostly members of the ruling elite—migrated annually.

However, most immigration into the United States has taken place since the Cuban Revolution. Between 1959 and the Cuban missile crisis of 1962 some 250,000 Cubans left the island. Between 1965 and 1973 some 300,000 Cubans—generally those with relatives in the United States—were allowed to leave on twice-daily flights between Varadero and Miami.

The next major wave of migration was in 1980. The "Mariel Boat Lift" saw 125,000 "Marielitos" leave Cuba either to join relatives or to pursue better economic prospects in the United States. They tended to belong to the working classes and were black or of mixed race rather than the white, wealthy Cubans of earlier migrations.

In 1990 Cuba's major supporter, the Soviet Union, collapsed. Cuba's economy suffered as a result and many Cubans have since tried to reach the United States. Using small boats, thousands have attempted to sail to Florida. Many have drowned in the process.

Areas of Settlement

The Cuban community of Miami is extremely well established and can cater to every aspect of Cuban life. Originally based in an area known as Little Havana in downtown Miami, it now extends beyond the city and throughout southern Florida. Despite having only 5 percent of the total Hispanic population, Miami is home to 20 of the largest Latino-owned businesses in the United States. Many newly arrived Cubans head straight for Miami because of family ties and business opportunities.

Elian Gonzalez

Elian Gonzalez was a five-year-old Cuban boy at the center of an international diplomatic storm in 1999. Along with his mother and her boyfriend, Elian was among a group of 14 refugees who set sail from Cuba on November 21 in a small aluminum boat to cross the 90 miles of ocean to Miami, Florida. The boat sank, and on November 25 Elian was found by the U.S. Coast Guard, clinging to an inner tube. He was one of only three survivors. He was placed with relatives in Miami who refused to return him to his father in Cuba despite being ordered to do so by the U.S. Immigration and Naturalization Service. A seven-month wrangle ensued before Elian was eventually reunited with his father in Cuba in June 2000.

A commercial fishing boat, overloaded with Cuban refugees, heads for Key West, Florida, from the Cuban port of Mariel.

Fact File: CUBANS

Distribution

Most populous states:
- Florida: 833,120, or 67%
- New Jersey: 77,337, or 6%
- California: 72,286, or 5.8%
- New York: 62,590, or 5%
- Texas: 25,705, or 2%
- Illinois: 18,438, or 1.5%

All 50 states have Cuban residents.

ILLINOIS · NEW YORK · CALIFORNIA · NEW JERSEY · TEXAS · FLORIDA

Region of origin

Cuba

The island of Cuba in the Caribbean, 90 miles south of the U.S. coast.

Population

1,241,685 (2000 U.S. census) = 0.4% of total population.

Jobs

Everything from lawyers and physicians to entrepreneurs, factory workers, and restaurant workers.

First immigrants

During the Ten Years' War (1868–1878) when Cuba fought against Spain.

Notable Cuban Americans

Desi Arnez, actor and musician most famous for the TV show *I Love Lucy*.

Gloria Estefan, singer.

Andy García, movie actor.

Oscar Hijuelos, writer.

César Romero, actor.

Useful websites

Cuba News—by CubaNet News Inc. (www.cubanet.org/cubanews.html)

United States and Cuba Sister Cities Association (www.uscsca.org)

Background on the U.S. Blockade (www.cubasolidarity.net/blockade.html)

The Complete Elian Gonzalez (www.thegully.com/essays/cuba/elian/completeelian.html)

Language

Spanish.

Names

Spanish surnames such as García and Rodriguez.

Community organizations

There are numerous political organizations agitating for Castro's removal, e.g., Cuban American National Foundation (www.canfnet.org/) and Cuban Representation of Exiles (www.cambiocubano.com/forcuba.html).

Others aim to help Cuban Americans, e.g., Cuban American National Council (www.cnc.org/) and Cuban American Legal Defense and Education Fund.

Religion

Catholicism (although 50 percent of Cubans have no religion).

Festivals

Cuba has many celebration days, most connected to the revolution, for example Liberation Day (January 1). In the United States anti-Castro feeling means these holidays are not observed by many Cuban Americans.

Food

Beans and rice (called *moros y cristianos* or Moors and Christians), *carne asada* (grilled meat), *fufú* (boiled green bananas). For dessert ice cream and *granizado* (shaved ice with sugary syrup).

Broadly speaking, Cuban Americans born in Cuba tend to be rather conservative. Many share a dislike of Fidel Castro and communism, they speak Spanish better than English and have more children than U.S.-born Cuban Americans. Their U.S.-born counterparts speak English rather than Spanish and are more likely to stay single or have smaller families. Cuban-born Cuban Americans are practicing Catholics, a religion outlawed by Castro in Cuba until 1998.

Cuban Americans are better educated than other Hispanic groups (in Cuba education is compulsory until the sixth grade, and literacy rates are very high), and as many as 47 percent of parents educate their children privately. Cuban Americans also enjoy a median income that is not far behind that of white Americans.

The Cuban American experience contains an inherent duality. They assimilate well into American society, they enjoy a comfortable standard of living, and they participate in American daily life (voter registration was 78 percent in 1989 and 1990, compared with 77.8 percent of white Americans). At the same time, they have long considered Cuba their home, and their ultimate goal is the overthrow of Castro and a return to Cuba. However, since the 1990s there has been a slight change as some Cubans have begun to see themselves as a minority group within the United States rather than an exile group who will be in the country only for the foreseeable future.

Arts, Culture, and Politics

Cubans preserve their culture when they move north. Cuban clubs and restaurants provide salsa music to dance to and Cuban food and drink such as rice, beans, and rum. Cuban singers like Gloria Estefan have gained popularity far beyond Cuba. Cubans tend to be fanatical baseball fans and follow their teams back on the island.

Politically most Cuban Americans, particularly those born in Cuba, are extremely aware. Most support the Republican Party, historically blaming the Democratic Party for the failure of the Bay of Pigs invasion in 1961, in which U.S.-backed rebels attempted to overthrow the communist government. Much of their political activity has been lobbying for the removal of Castro and his regime. However, Cuban Americans are also involved in local politics and have elected Cuban representatives to the U.S. Congress, like Florida Republican Lincoln Diaz-Balart and Robert Menendez, the first Cuban American Democrat to represent New Jersey.

Trade with Cuba

Since the Cuban Revolution of 1959 the United States has imposed trade and travel sanctions on Cuba. The trade embargo was announced in 1960, and it banned all U.S. exports to Cuba, except for foodstuffs, medicines, and medical and hospital supplies. However, Cuba and Canada carry on active trade, with many Canadians visiting the island, despite the American boycott. Cuban immigration to Canada also takes place.

See Also

- The Cold War and ethnicity (Volume 2)
- Hispanic Americans (Volume 5)
- Illegal immigration (Volume 5)
- Industry and employment (Volume 5)

A Cuban market displays Cuban music, foods, and other goods in Calle Ocho, Little Havana, Miami, Florida.

Cultural borderlands form in places where two or more different cultures meet. The term "culture" in this sense refers to the inherited ideas, beliefs, and values that bind a particular group of people together and create their sense of identity, but it also describes their social and artistic expression—in language, customs, food, music, and art. Culture is defined by ethnic origin but is also influenced by social, economic, and political factors.

The borderlands between different cultures coincide both with national boundaries—for example, the frontier between the United States and Mexico—and on a local level, with less formal boundaries between different communities in the same country, such as the streets separating a Hispanic urban neighborhood from a black or a Chinese one. Borders can be interpreted as being both the edges of separate communities and also the meeting points between them. They are the places where people from different cultural backgrounds come into contact and interact on a direct, daily basis. Sometimes the result of this "cultural mingling" is a new hybrid culture that contains elements of the different cultures that created it but is quite distinct from them. In any country, but especially one as multicultural as the United States, cultural borderlands play a significant part in the acceptance and interaction of immigrant groups in wider society.

Two Jewish men eating Chinese food prepared according to kosher guidelines in a restaurant in New York City. Restaurants, bars, stores, schools, and churches are some of the cultural borderlands in which cultural interaction between different groups first takes place.

Native American Borderlands

European settlers first came into contact with Native Americans in the 16th century. While relations between the two groups were sometimes amicable, they were increasingly marked by hostility and warfare as the Europeans forcibly took ownership of Native American lands. Many Native Americans were forced to move to reservations. Later, in the 19th century European culture was imposed on Native American culture. In the 1880s the U.S. government forced many Native Americans to relocate from their reservations in an attempt to assimilate them into U.S. society. The government also took Native American youths from their homes and made them attend white-run schools. These acts helped undermine the Native American communities and their culture. Today Native Americans have more rights. Tribes live on large reservations and continue to preserve their own traditions of religion, language, and medicine.

The United States and Mexico

The physical borderland between the United States and Mexico has produced a number of distinct cultural forms that many have come to identify, at their most specific, as "Tex-Mex" or in their most general form as "Southwestern." They are the result of centuries of interaction between the many diverse communities that have settled in the area: principally Native Americans, Mexican Indians, and Spanish and British colonists. The manifestations of this cultural borderland include "Tex-Mex" food—a spicy combination of traditional Mexican, Hispanic, and British dishes—and "Conjunto" music, a blend of traditional Mexican and European music centered around the accordion, guitar, and drum, and popularized by musicians such as Santiago "El Flaco" Jimenez. Other examples include the Southwestern pop music of stars like Selena, the

performance art of artists such as Guillermo Gómez Peña (for example, his *Border Brujo*), and novels like Rudolfo Anaya's award-winning *Bless Me, Ultima*. The unique hybrid culture of the region is also seen in its employment patterns, such as the *maquiladoras* (assembly plants) that pepper the United States–Mexico border.

Urban Borderlands

While the cultural borderlands found in cities like New York, Chicago, and Los Angeles are not as clearly defined as national boundaries, they are places of just as much cultural exchange. There different types of people come into constant contact with one another—in their home neighborhood, their workplace, and public spaces like schools, churches, stores, malls, restaurants, and cafes. Since most people are drawn to cities in search of work and a better way of life, the workplace can be a key location for cultural mingling. This mingling can have both positive and negative results in multicultural cities. For example, in the textile factories of Lower Eastside, New York City, in the 1940s poor working conditions and pay led female garment

Guillermo Gómez Peña

Guillermo Gómez Peña (1955–) is an award-winning Mexican poet, playwright, and performance artist, born in Mexico City but currently based in San Francisco, California. He uses his body and language to challenge the conventions of culture, class, and race. His performance work *Border Brujo* saw him dressed in sombrero, a wrestler mask, dark glasses, skeleton earrings, feathers, and a necklace of plastic bananas. His view is that such costumes mirror the disjunctive experience of living on or near the U.S–Mexican border and reflect the cultural stereotypes to be found there.

Men and women work at tables in a maquiladora *(assembly plant) in Tijuana, Baja California, Mexico. This is just one of many* maquiladora *facilities located in the U.S. border zone of northern Mexico that manufacture finished goods for export to the United States. The plants are generally owned by non-Mexican corporations and take advantage of plentiful low-cost Mexican labor, advantageous tariff regulations, and their close proximity to markets in the United States to produce goods such as home appliances and automobiles. In 1999 more than 3,500 plants employed approximately 1.2 million workers.*

Female workers at a shirt factory in New York City in the late 1930s. By the 1940s and 1950s U.S. garment workers from a variety of ethnic backgrounds had united to become highly unionized. Wages were at an all-time high. The U.S. industry suffered decline from the 1960s onward as cheaper labor supplies were utilized in countries such as Mexico.

See also

- Cultural mingling (Volume 3)
- Cultural retention (Volume 3)
- Illegal immigration (Volume 5)
- Immigrant experience (Volume 5)
- Intermarriage (Volume 5)
- Multiple ethnic origins (Volume 7)
- Nativism (Volume 8)
- Segregation and integration (Volume 9)
- Urban reform and race (Volume 10)

workers from different communities—Jewish, Italian, Irish, black, Puerto Rican, and Cuban—to unite in the struggle for a better deal. On the other hand, competition for work can increase cultural division, particularly in times of economic downturn. At such times the gap between rich and poor often becomes more pronounced, and interracial tension, crime, and violence increase. Such a development occurred in Los Angeles in the 1980s and 1990s. Some wealthier communities in the city chose to live in compounds protected by fortified walls, gates, and security guards. In effect they closed the cultural borderlands between themselves and other communities, a trend that has worried many social observers.

Schools can also be significant places of cultural mingling. Their intake often includes pupils from many different communities. This can enable children to learn about different cultures but can also result in lower test scores if, for example, not all pupils share the same first language. This combination of benefit and disadvantage is typical of cultural borderlands. Other key sites for cultural exchange and acceptance are food stores, cafes, and restaurants. Foods of specific ethnic origin such as the bagel, pizza, and taco have now become ubiquitous throughout the United States. In some cases the urban communities that first produced them have themselves become cultural borderlands, a phenomenon most evident in many American "Chinatowns." In Los Angeles, for example, the area known as Chinatown is full of restaurants that cater to an American idea of Chinese food and culture, while the Chinese themselves have moved away to live in other suburbs.

Cultural mingling

The process of cultural mingling occurs when two or more cultures come into contact and interact with one another. North America is a perfect example of cultural mingling, with culturally diverse groups from all over the world meeting on one continent. The term "melting pot" has also been used to describe this phenomenon.

Colonization and Cultural Exchange

Before 1492 and the beginning of European colonization cultural mingling took place between the many diverse groups of Native American peoples. After 1492 a different type of cultural interaction took place in North America, as groups of people from a different continent arrived with their own cultures, beliefs, and values. During this period the process of cultural mingling became defined by the attempts of European colonists to displace and dominate Native American peoples. It was also marked by the colonists' efforts to dominate the African slaves whom they imported to work in their plantations, farmlands, and homes. Such forcible and unequal cultural exchange remained a dominant force in the history of America—and many other nations—for centuries. However, even out of such negative relationships new "hybrid" cultural practices and beliefs emerged that combined elements from both cultures to create something new. Examples include language ("pidgin," or simplified versions of English or French) and religions combining African spirituality with Christianity (Santeria Lucumi, Coromble, and Voodoo).

In addition to exploitation, more positive aspects of cultural mingling occurred during the European colonization of North America. Many different peoples were attracted to North America, most in search of a new life and opportunities, but some fleeing persecution in their own countries. While they all shared a common European ancestry, each group brought its own distinct national traditions, beliefs, languages, music, food, and art. In a period when most ordinary people did not travel far from their local village or town, their arrival in America was often the first time that they had come into contact with a culture other than their own—even if it was another European culture.

The degree to which these peoples interacted and exchanged cultural ideas and practices was often determined both

Useful websites

Searchable dictionary of Pidgin English (www.e-hawaii.com/fun/pidgin/default.asp)
The African American Collection of articles published by the B. Davis Schwartz Memorial Library of Long Island University summarizing American slavery (www.cwpost.liunet.edu/cwis/cwp/library/aaslavry.htm)
The Impact of Globalization The effects of economic liberalization and globalization with specific examples from the impact on India and Asia (http://members.tripod.com/~INDIA_RESOURCE/globalization.html)

Two American families greet each other in their backyard. Friendship and interaction between neighboring communities, whether in the home, workplace, or public areas, is at the heart of cultural mingling.

33

The Black Panthers march in New York City in 1968 to protest against the trial for murder of one of their members, Huey P. Newton.

by their own cultures and by the practicalities of daily life in a new land. When peoples mix freely and exchange and modify their behavior, beliefs, and customs in response to other cultures and the environment in which they find themselves, the process is termed "assimilation." The desire of immigrants or their descendants to retain the culture of their homeland is termed "cultural retention." Both tendencies are fundamental to the identity of a person and the community of which they are part. However, they can also create tensions in a multicultural society between maintaining the identities of individual groups and creating an overall society in which they can all coexist and share a common set of beliefs and values.

Mobility and Mass Media

In the closing decades of the 20th century two developments emerged that have had a huge impact on cultural mingling. The availability of comparatively cheap airline flights, both national and inter-continental, has dramatically increased many people's mobility. People now travel much more extensively than ever before, for their vacations and their work, bringing them into contact with new places, situations, and cultures. The process of cultural mingling has also been accelerated by developments in the mass media, particularly television and the Internet. They have meant that different peoples throughout the world are brought into contact with cultures other than their own without even setting foot outside their homes. People can encounter and be influenced by "foreign" cultures without coming into direct physical contact with them. Mobility and mass media are both key factors in the trend toward "globalization," that is, thinking about things in worldwide rather than national terms.

Cultural Tension and Gangs

Despite the general trend toward greater cultural mingling, however, certain factors can lead to tension between different cultural groups. Probably the most significant of these factors are poverty and competition for work—as they are in wider society. Competition can easily turn to rivalry and hostility, as communities seek to protect their own interests or become jealous of communities that appear more successful. Fights between gangs from different ethnic groups and communities are the clearest examples of this cultural tension. For example, in the late 19th and early 20th centuries there was a series of territorial battles between rival Chinese secret societies in Chicago and New York, among other cities, which became known as the "Tong Wars." Gang warfare continues today in many urban areas, and tension between different ethnic communities contributed to the 1992 riots in Los Angeles.

The "Power" Movements

The political struggles of the 1950s and 1960s prompted an extremely rich period of cultural mingling that produced many youth movements in the United States. They asserted their right to equality—both racial and sexual—and their campaigning brought about a permanent change in the way people viewed themselves in relation to the nation or the government. Among the many groups involved in this Civil Rights movement were the Black Power movement, the Puerto Rican Young Lords Organization, the Chicano or Mexican American Brown Berets, the American Indian Movement, the Chinese American Red Dragons, and the Anglo American Appalachian Young Patriots.

Music and Cultural Exchange

Cultural mingling has been at the root of most popularized art forms, especially music. New types of music have emerged as musicians and singers from different cultures and backgrounds have worked together. For example, salsa is an amalgamation of many different musical traditions, including the Cuban Son Montuno, the Puerto Rican Bomba, and African American jazz.

Music in the United States has always been a product of interactions between different ethnic groups. The music of the 1940s and 1950s helped establish a black renaissance in the arts, with leading artists like Dizzy Gillespie, Mario Bauza, Tito Puente, Frank "Machito" Grillo, Luciano "Chano" Pozo y Gonzales, Nat "King" Cole, Charlie Parker, Pablo "Tito" Rodriguez, Xavier Cugat, Ramon "Mongo" Santamaria, Perez Prado, Celia

Jimi Hendrix

Born in Seattle, Hendrix was mainly raised by his father, who bought him his first guitar at age 16. Jimi was briefly in the army before going on the road as a backup musician for artists like Little Richard and Jackie Wilson. In 1966 he was "discovered" by Chas Chandler and taken to England, where he formed a trio with bassist Noel Redding and drummer Mitch Mitchell. He became an immediate success within the psychedelic movement. His albums and live performances are part of music legend. He performed his last concert in Germany in 1970. He died two weeks later from barbiturate intoxication at the age of 27.

The popular Cuban musician and bandleader Perez Pantalon Prado, shown here in 1955 posing with a congo drum.

See Also

- Art (Volume 1)
- Assimilation (Volume 1)
- Cultural borderlands (Volume 3)
- Cultural retention (Volume 3)
- Immigrant experience (Volume 5)
- Intermarriage (Volume 5)
- Music (Volume 7)

Cruz, Bo Diddley, the Harptones, the Vocaleers, Frankie Lymon, Ruth Brown, Stan Getz, Antonio Carlos Jobim, Astrud Gilberto, and Cal Tjader. Not only were new types of music like soul, jazz, and salsa created, but they also attracted an increasingly wide audience drawn from right across society.

Equally, in the 1960s and 1970s artists from many ethnic backgrounds produced politicized music that expressed the concerns of the civil rights movement. Musicians such as Jimi Hendrix, Carlos Santana, the Temptations, War, and Sly and the Family Stone sang about issues that concerned much of the United States—issues of citizenship, human rights, multiculturalism, and a host of other political subjects.

New types of music continue to emerge from cultural mingling in North America. Hip-hop culture and "rap" music are a result of the continuous cultural interactions between African Americans, Puerto Ricans, West Indians, and others in urban areas such as the Bronx, New York, in the late 1970s and early 1980s. They involve young people from diverse economic backgrounds, from middle-income families to gangs such as Zulu Nation and Tough Bronx Action. Hip-hop culture, its dress, dance, slang, body language, and art, has become a central part of youth culture across the world.

A Living Tradition

The strong tradition of cultural mingling that has shaped North American society over the centuries is a constant and ever-changing process. The 20th century saw major advances toward achieving equality for all American citizens—whatever their race or sex—and was also a time when people's awareness of different cultures increased with developments in mass media and transport. There is also evidence that certain ethnic groups, such as third-generation Mexican Americans, increasingly are marrying people from outside their own cultural group. These advances continue to shape patterns of cultural intermingling in the 21st century, and despite tensions between different ethnic communities, they provide positive opportunities for cultural interaction.

Cultural retention

When an immigrant group or individual in a new society holds onto his or her native heritage, this is known as cultural retention. It is a common strategy used by both national and individual ethnic communities in an attempt to define their communal experience. Many groups seek to retain their cultural identities as a means of maintaining their connection to their ancestral past and as an aid to shaping their future identity. Identity—whether individual or communal—is constantly being renegotiated in response to the forces of history and of the dominant prevailing culture. Therefore, maintaining one's cultural identity is a struggle that requires a continuing commitment to resist complete assimilation.

Historical Perspectives

For any nation-state it is important to maintain a cultural base that, while it retains some aspects of the past, is flexible enough to respond to the challenges and changes that are part of every vibrant society. So this type of national cultural retention must inform a nation's historical narrative as well as its development in the future. For example, many citizens of the United States proclaim a national allegiance based on an ideal of the country's "forefathers"—wealthy white English-speaking males—alongside such nation-building texts as the Bill of Rights and the Constitution. However, when confronted with the contradictions of 21st-century American society, people can hold up the country's social history and development—from its origins as a British colony through its foundations as a plantation slave economy to its current manifestation as a "multicultural" society—as a way of explaining the nation's disproportionate allocation of social advantages based on race, ethnicity, class, gender, sexuality, and age. While maintenance of cultural forms can be seen as an important influence on social continuity, retention of those cultural forms could be said at the same time to be a hindrance to assimilation and cultural homogenization, which are also necessary

A man displays his Italian American pride at the Columbus Day Parade, St. Louis, Missouri, in October 1991.

A tepee set up outside the Bureau of Indian Affairs in Washington, D.C., in November 1972 to protest against government treatment of Native Americans. Much U.S. government legislation over a long period had sought to assimilate Native American peoples into the mainstream by denying them the right to retain and celebrate their traditional cultures.

Useful websites

La Alianza Hispana (The Hispanic Alliance) (www.laalianza. org/main.htm)
The Latino News Network (www.latnn.com)
Aboriginal Connections: USA (www.aboriginalconnections.com/ links/United_States_of_America)
Columbus Day (www.holidayfestival.com/ individual/ColumbusDay.html)

to build a stable community in a land of diverse ethnic groupings. In fact, within North America the experiences of working peoples—particularly peoples of color, such as Native Americans, African Americans, Latinos, and Asian Americans—stand out as examples of cultural retention used as a tool of resistance and survival.

The First Peoples

The Native American community in North America, despite in many cases having been removed from its ancestral homelands by the U.S. government, has maintained cultural practices that predate the arrival of Europeans. Such cultural practices as "pow-wows" and "sweats" have endured despite the incursions and restrictions placed on Native American cultures by incoming settlers and governmental agencies like the United States Bureau of Indian Affairs. The United States' policy of "Manifest Destiny" in the mid-19th century allowed the United States to expand its borders from coast to coast, often to the detriment of the many Native American peoples already living there. This expansion of territory required the United States to diminish the Native American presence through forced relocation to Indian Reservations or the signing of treaties that restricted Native American influence in what had traditionally been their homelands. Native American peoples continue to use ancient cultural forms to give their community a point of historic origin on which to base their shared identity, and in so doing they retain a means of remembering and honoring their past history.

The African American Experience

Rather like Native American peoples, the African American community, after the violent break with their homeland through the slave trade of the 18th and 19th centuries, has retained many of the cultural forms of its African roots. They have, in many cases, been combined with new cultural practices conceived within North America. Examples might range from the adoption of dance moves that have a direct relation to their African origins to the value placed on improvisation in both poetry and new musical genres, such as blues, jazz, rhythm and blues, and hip-hop. African culture has flourished in many ways within the United States despite the restrictions and obstacles it has faced since the arrival of the first slaves right through to the Civil Rights era of the 1960s. Present-day cultural practices, such as the Baptist tradition of worship and many forms of popular music and dance, can be linked to their "roots" in Africa, demonstrating the power of cultural retention.

Maintaining Ethnic Cultures

The most common strategy of resistance to the pressures of assimilating to U.S. culture is the maintenance of one's ethnic culture. Culture used as a weapon is an important idea because the values or lifestyle of an ethnic group have the potential to undermine the "power" of the dominant group. Music, poetry, or other popular cultural traditions provide communities with a way to get closer to the origins of their identity.

The expression of ethnic identity through art and music places one's notions of the past, the present, or a possible future within a continuous dialogue. A group or community may take their identity from the past, but this identity is ultimately defined by their contemporary experience. Thus the significance of the past is always changing to suit the needs of the present. In the use of dress, language, food, art, or other cultural practices the definitions of community are challenged, or identity is reaffirmed. For instance, various Latino groups, as they have ascended up the social or political ladders of the United States, have established multiple cultural outlets. These outlets range from ethnic parades to the nationally recognized Hispanic Heritage Month in November. In maintaining their cultural identities within the cultural maelstrom of the United States "melting pot," Latino people have made concentrated efforts to establish institutions or centers of learning and cultural maintenance. These cultural centers initially

The salsa is a popular dance form with many Latino immigrants to the United States and represents one way of retaining contact with their cultural roots.

sprang from small beginnings. Often people would maintain their cultures via simple meetings where ideas would be exchanged. Cultural forms such as music, poetry, philosophy, and history, remained vibrant in the lives of both newly arrived and established Latinos, as seen through activities such as impromptu political caucuses, church or community celebrations or events, poetry slams, or musical jam sessions. As Civil Rights legislation extended to include Latinos in the 1960s, funding for Latino arts increased. As a result, Latino communities within the United States began to establish cultural institutions requiring state funding to ensure their cultural survival. In the United States these institutions have been instrumental in legitimizing not only Latin American art, but also the art produced within the United States by the many Latino communities living here. A multitude of county museums, universities, and state or city buildings have displayed exhibits or housed performances coming from the Latino community, which taken together express a developing sense of Latino identity.

"Latinidad" or "Latinismo"

These words have been coined to express a new idea of Latin identity that was born in the late 20th century. Moving into the new millennium, there has been a reevaluation of the definition of what it means to be part of the Latino community in the United States. "Latinidad" is a generationally defined political-cultural identity that often takes on the more popular structures of music, dress, dance, and language as they apply to Latinos in the United States. Thus we see the institutionalization of certain music types, such as salsa, tango, samba, lambada, rancheras, merengue, or banda, as specifically "Latino," when in reality their creation might be either more multicultural or more culturally specific in origin.

Conversely, Latinos' contributions to other musical or dance forms, such as soul, hip-hop, pop, jazz, house, disco, boogaloo, or the hustle, have become relegated to the margins of public knowledge since it has been convenient for those forms to be exclusively labeled as creations of the African American community. The reality of being part of the Latino community in the United States is that while Latino people have their own individualized ethnic, racial, or class identities, by politically or culturally aligning themselves with a broader Latino community, they are able to bring a collective power to their continuing struggle for human and civil rights.

Controversial rapper and musician Ice Cube, seen in 2000. He has pushed back musical boundaries and incorporated aspects from different cultures into his performance.

Maintaining Native Cultures

New immigrants, such as those from the former Soviet Union, the African continent, and parts of Asia, Europe, and Latin America, hold true to the North American tradition carried on through the centuries by all immigrant groups to the region by continuing to maintain their "native culture" within their newly adopted home—the United States. Their struggles against cultural homogenization and the total loss of their past can be seen in their communal efforts to establish ethnic-specific annual parades, strengthen bilingual education programs in the United States, and guarantee access to resources across any linguistic or cultural barriers. Cultural retention continues to act as a survival tool for foreign-born newcomers, legal residents, and domestic-born citizens alike. So, while it is not uncommon to see Italian American pride flourish on October 12—Columbus Day—and to see the Chinese American community gather during the Chinese New Year, the emergence of new ethnic celebrations is not at all surprising. Many of these days of ethnic pride often represent national days of independence from a particular group's homeland, or sometimes they are randomly chosen in relation to the United States' calendar of federally recognized public holidays.

The Chinese New Year Parade held in Chinatown, San Francisco, California, is an important example of cultural retention in practice.

Individual Cultural Expressions

Other instances of cultural retention can take place on the individual level. They might translate into people expressing their particular ethnic or racial identity for the first time within a cultural community or form, exploring aspects of their background that may hitherto have lain hidden. Examples of this type of crosscultural interaction can be found in such notable cultural figures as Jimi Hendrix, Ella Fitzgerald, Nat King Cole, Desi Arnaz, Jr., Tito Puente, and Ice Cube. These performers have pushed the boundaries of their recognized ethnic identities—and their corresponding stereotypes—and laid claim to all the types of cultural forms that make up their identities. These individual examples illustrate the past meeting the present to challenge our future vision of what is legitimate and what might be labeled as unacceptable or abnormal. Cultural retention, utilized constructively, can serve as a tool of education and multicultural understanding and communal unity.

See also

- Cultural borderlands (Volume 3)
- Cultural mingling (Volume 3)
- Language retention (Volume 6)
- Nativism (Volume 8)

According to the 2000 U.S. census, there are approximately 1.4 million people of Czech descent living in the United States. This is the largest Czech community outside of the present day Czech Republic, which has a population of 10 million. Czech immigration to North America has advanced in waves beginning in the 19th century. The most recent wave accompanied the collapse of communism in 1989 and the breakup of Czechoslovakia in 1993.

Significant Czech communities can be found in Nebraska, Iowa, Minnesota, Wisconsin, Texas, and North and South Dakota, as well as in the cities of New York, Chicago, and Cleveland. Canada also has a sizable Czech population, with communities concentrated in Montreal and Winnipeg. The Czech community has been very well assimilated. As a result, many second- or third-generation Czechs are unfamiliar with the language and history of their ancestors.

History of Immigration

In the mid-1800s the Czech provinces of Bohemia, Moravia, and Silesia were part of the Austro-Hungarian Empire. In 1848 Czechs were defeated in the Prague uprising against Austrian rule, and a stream of Czech political refugees started arriving in New York. In 1862 the Homestead Act attracted Czech farmers and villagers to the American Midwest by offering free land to those who would agree to become U.S. citizens. As economic conditions deteriorated at home in the 1870s, skilled workers including miners, tailors, shoemakers, and carpenters joined Czech farmers in establishing a new life in the United States. Between 1848 and 1918, 350,000 Czechs came to the United States in pursuit of economic and political freedom.

Additional waves of immigration continued throughout the 20th century with the collapse of the Austro-Hungarian Empire and the creation of an independent Czecho-slovakia in 1918. However, many Czechs did return to the newly independent state in the years that followed. By 1920 the U.S. census reported that more than 600,000 Americans claimed Czech as their native language. With Nazi Germany's occupation of Czechoslovakia in 1938, emigration increased again. In 1968 the Soviet invasion of Czechoslovakia led to another wave of Czech immigration to North America. The most recent wave occurred in the 1990s as a result of the collapse of communism in 1989 and the subsequent breakup of Czechoslovakia into two states on January 1, 1993.

Notable Czech Americans

Madaleine Albright, politician.

Nicole Bobek, figure skater.

Milos Forman, film director.

Tomas Garrigue Masaryk (first president of independent Czechoslovakia. His wife, Charlotte Garrigue, was an American).

Martina Navratilova, tennis champion.

Czech women and their children sit on the deck of an immigrant ship in 1920. They are about to disembark at Ellis Island, New York, to be processed by immigration officials.

Distribution

Based on 2000 U.S. census total of 1.4 million, the most populous states are:
- Texas: 208,518, or 14.8%
- Illinois: 155,868, or 11%
- Wisconsin: 91,182, or 6.5%
- Ohio: 83,451, or 5.9%
- Nebraska: 78,718, or 5.6%
- Minnesota: 78,710, or 5.6%
- New York: 78,534, or 5.6%
- Iowa: 49,747, or 3.5%

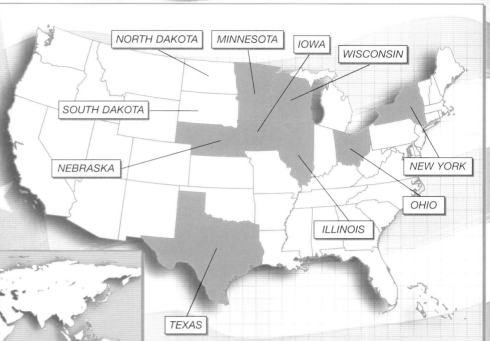

NORTH DAKOTA · MINNESOTA · IOWA · WISCONSIN · SOUTH DAKOTA · NEBRASKA · NEW YORK · OHIO · ILLINOIS · TEXAS

Region of origin

Czech Republic

Formerly Czechoslovakia (1918–1993) in Central Europe. Since 1993 it has become two independent countries: the Czech Republic and Slovakia.

Population

1.4 million according to 2000 U.S. Census.

Language

English and Czech.

First immigrants

1633. The earliest known immigrant, Augustin Herman, helped found the Virginia tobacco trade in the 17th century. The earliest wave of immigrants came to the United States in the mid-1800s, fleeing economic and political persecution under Austrian rule. (The Czech lands of Bohemia, Moravia, and Silesia were at that time part of the Austro-Hungarian Empire.)

Dates of major arrivals

- Mid-1800s: Following Austria crushing the Czech uprising.
- 1919–1939: In the years between the world wars.
- 1968: Following the Soviet invasion of Czechoslovakia.
- Post-1989: Following the collapse of communism in Europe.

Most populous cities

New York City; Chicago, Illinois; Cleveland, Ohio.

Jobs

Small business owners, professionals, farmers, skilled workers such as butchers, carpenters, shoemakers, and tailors.

Names

Novak, Novotny, Svoboda, Dvorak, Cerny, and Zeman. Female names end in –ova. For example, Mr. Navratil, Ms. Navratilova ("–ova" means either "daughter of" or "wife of").

Community organizations

Czech Heritage Preservation Society (www.czechs.org/)
Czech and Slovak Heritage Association (www.czechheritage.net/)
Czech and Slovak Genealogical Society International (www.cgsi.org/)
Czechoslovak Society of Arts and Sciences (www.svu2000.org/)
American Sokol (www.american-sokol.org/)

Religion

Predominantly Roman Catholic.

Festivals

Several heritage festivals are arranged each year in Czech communities throughout the United States. They include polka festivals and *kolache* festivals. (*Kolache* is a Czech wedding pastry. *Kolache* festivals celebrate all aspects of Czech culture.)

Food

Pork and *knedliky* (dumplings) or potatoes (boiled or baked).

See also

• The Cold War and ethnicity
  (Volume 1)
• Emigrés and refugees (Volume 4)
• Immigrant experience (Volume 5)
• Slovaks (Volume 9)

Madaleine Albright

Madaleine Albright was born in 1937 in Prague, Czechoslovakia, to a Czech diplomat and his wife. Albright first came to the United States at the age of 11 when the communists came to power in Czechoslovakia in 1948. Albright served as the U.S. permanent representative to the United Nations from 1993 to 1997. In 1997 she was sworn in as the first female secretary of state in U.S. history. During her tenure with the Clinton administration she oversaw the entrance of the Czech Republic into the North Atlantic Treaty Organization (NATO).

Education and Lifestyle

Czechs place a high value on education and have worked hard to build schools in their communities. It is estimated that 97 percent of Czech immigrants arriving in the United States during the 20th century were literate. According to the 1990 U.S. census, 30 percent of Czechs in America had a bachelor's degree or higher. More than 60 percent of those who claim Czech ancestry work in managerial, professional, technical, sales, and administrative positions, with 5 percent remaining in farming and related industries.

Fewer than 10 percent of Czechs in the United States speak a language other than English. Czechs celebrate all the major American holidays, but incorporate traditional Czech food and music into the festivities. There are a number of newsletters, circulated by organizations such as the Czech Center of New York, that keep Czech Americans informed of upcoming heritage festivals, cultural events, and other activities.

Culture and Politics

Czechs are among the world's greatest composers and artists. Among recent artists Czech director Milos Forman has gained respect and acclaim for his film career. Forman, whose American films include *One Flew Over the Cuckoo's Nest* (1975), *Hair* (1979), *Amadeus* (1984), *The People vs. Larry Flynt* (1996), and *Man on the Moon* (1999), has won multiple Oscars for his work.

Czechs have contributed a great deal to sports in North America, especially soccer, tennis, hockey, and skating. An organization called *Sokol* (Falcon), established in St. Louis, Missouri, in 1865, remains an important factor in promoting both Czech cultural life in America and also the Czech Republic as a nation.

Czechs in the United States have taken an active interest in the politics of their homeland dating back to World War I (1914–1918), when they raised money to support Czechoslovak independence. The independence movement was led by Czech émigré Tomas Garrigue Masaryk, who was married to an American, Charlotte Garrigue. Masaryk spent much of 1918 in the United States lobbying and negotiating for the creation of an independent Czechoslovak state. Upon achieving this goal in October 1918, Masaryk was elected Czechoslovakia's first president.

The organization American Friends of the Czech Republic has been particularly active in promoting cooperation between the United States and Czech lands. Given the Czech Republic's emergence from communism in the early 1990s and activities designed to further integrate the country into Western institutions, it is likely that ties between Czechs in America and the Czech Republic will continue to strengthen in the future.

Danes

Despite its low profile, Danish immigrant history maintains a subtle yet significant presence in America. During the past 350 years more than 500,000 Danes have emigrated to the United States, and the country of Denmark continues to maintain strong connections with America. A distinctly Danish presence is found in communities located largely in the Midwestern states of Iowa, Wisconsin, Minnesota, Utah, and Nebraska, as well as in California, Oregon, and Washington. While the lifestyle of the earliest Danish communities can now be seen only in museums and heritage sites, contemporary Danish culture is expressed in various celebrations and is often associated with religious and social organizations. There are about 90,000 people of Danish origin in Canada, mainly in Ontario, Alberta, and British Columbia. Danish immigrants and their descendants in the United States and Canada have made significant contributions in many fields, including the dairy industry, market gardening, and the cooperative movement.

The Pattern of Danish Immigration

The first recorded Dane in North America was the 17th-century explorer Jens Munk, who reached Hudson Bay in 1619. Danish immigrants soon followed, among them Jonas Bronck, who in 1629 bought farmland in New York that later became the city's Bronx neighborhood—although some scholars now think that Bronck might have been Swedish. Early settlement by Danes was sporadic and scattered. However, from 1850 the number of Danes emigrating to North America steadily increased. In that year Mormon missionaries from Utah arrived in Denmark, and many Danish converts emigrated to settle in small farming communities in the state. The 1862 Homestead Act, which opened up land for immigrants from various European nations, stimulated a further increase in Danish emigration. Thousands of Danes took advantage of the opportunity, many because they had lost real estate in Schleswig and Holstein when Denmark was forced to surrender the regions to Prussia in 1864. By the 1890s most Danish emigrants came to the United States for economic rather than religious or political reasons, as a rising population put pressure on the Danish economy. They were further encouraged by the advertising of emigration agents.

Danish immigrants came from areas and islands throughout Denmark. They settled in cities, including New York, Chicago, Racine, Minneapolis, Omaha, Portland, and Seattle, although their presence is most

Notable Danish Americans

Victor Borge (1909–2000), musician and entertainer.

Gutzon Borglum (1867–1941), sculptor who carved the Mount Rushmore memorial.

Jacob Riis (1849–1914), journalist and social commentator.

Peter Sørensen (1854–1929), church leader and teacher.

Examples of Danish architecture in downtown Solvang, California, the "Danish capital of America." The settlement was founded by Danish educators in 1911.

Most populous states:
• Iowa
• Wisconsin
• Nebraska
• Minnesota
• Utah
• California

Most populous cities:
• New York
• Chicago
• Los Angeles
• San Francisco

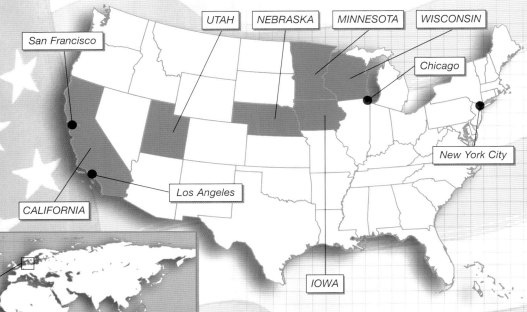

San Francisco

UTAH NEBRASKA MINNESOTA WISCONSIN

Chicago

CALIFORNIA

Los Angeles

New York City

IOWA

Region of origin

Denmark

Denmark is a small independent country in the region of northern Europe called Scandinavia.

Population

According to the 2000 U.S. census: 882,474.

Language

Danish and English.

Community organizations

Danish Brotherhood in America (www.danishbrotherhood.org/)
Danish Sisterhood in America (www.danishsisterhood.org/)
Danish American Heritage Society (www.dana.edu/dahs/)
Danish American Chamber of Commerce (www.daccny.com/)
Danish American Society (www.das–ny.org/)

Dates of major arrivals

• 1850s: The arrival in Denmark of Mormon missionaries from Utah in 1850 led to the first significant increase in Danish emigration.
• 1860–1880s: The number of emigrants was swelled by America's Homestead Act (1862), which created opportunities to buy land, and by the loss of Danish territories in Schleswig-Holstein (1864).
• 1890s–1910s: A growing population and economic pressures in Denmark led to a further increase in emigration to the United States.

Jobs

The majority of early Danish immigrants in the United States worked in agriculture, particularly dairy farming. They also worked in construction, factories, domestic service, trades, the clergy, and social services. Today Danes work in a wide range of occupations.

First immigrants

Jens Munk (1579–1628) a Danish explorer reached North America in 1619. He and his men celebrated the first Lutheran Christmas service on the continent near what is now called Hudson Bay.

Religion

Most Danish Americans are Lutheran Christians. There is also a Danish Mormon community in Utah.

Festivals

All major Christian festivals, especially Christmas.
Grundlovsdag, or Constitution Day (June 5).
Rebildfest (July 4). This is an unusual festival because it is held in Denmark to celebrate American Independence Day. It is the largest such celebration held outside the United States and is attended by many Danish Americans.

Names

Andersen, Beck, Christensen, Dam, Hansen, Jensen, Larsen, Nielsen, Overgaard, and Rasmussen.

Food

Cookies, filled pastries, *æbleskiver* (pancakes), *smørrebrød* (open sandwiches), pork, *frikadeller* (meatballs), seafood, and *brunede kartofler* (potatoes fried in butter and sugar).

evident in the settlement of prairie lands and small towns in America's heartland. The most recent wave of Danish immigrants came to the United States in the 1950s and 1960s. They were mostly highly educated young professionals who settled in major cities like New York, Chicago, Los Angeles, and San Francisco.

Economic Contribution

Danes came to the United States for numerous reasons. Many looked to America as a land of economic opportunity where the trades and crafts they learned in Europe could make vital contributions to economic development in new communities. In the mid-19th century Midwestern states were opened and cleared for farms, towns, and cities, and Danes were recruited to work the land, construct buildings, and process the produce from the dairies and farms in the new states.

As Danish American communities developed, a progressive social consciousness influenced Danish ministers, teachers, writers, and social reformers to come to the United States, first to meet the spiritual needs and address the social problems of Danes in America, and later to contribute to American communities. During the period from 1864 to 1914 more than 250,000 Danes immigrated. Today, America continues to attract the highest number of Danish emigrants.

Danish Assimilation

Early Danish immigrants found it relatively easy to assimilate into their new nation. The Danish language is structured in a similar way to English, and the immigrants' children easily learned the new language in their schools and communities. Despite a willingness to assimilate, many Danes retained a distinctive ethnic identity. They were aided and encouraged by the 19th-century Danish religious leader and social reformer Frederik Lange Grundtvig , who helped found Grand View College in Des Moines, Iowa, and the Dansk Folkes-amfund (Danish Folk Society). His work contributed to the development of Danish Lutheran churches and the establishment of Danish folk schools in North America. Within these educational, religious, and cultural institutions Danish immigrants found a way to express their Danish American identity.

Victor Borge

Victor Borge (1909–2000) was born in Copenhagen, Denmark, and educated at the Royal Danish Academy of Music. During the 1930s Borge became known as one of the most popular musicians in Denmark. He began mixing humor with his performances and became a performer and comedian in film and radio. Blacklisted by the occupying force of Nazis, he was forced to leave Denmark in 1940. Borge settled in the United States and became a citizen in 1948. He performed as a piano soloist and conductor with numerous orchestras and continued to blend music with humor throughout his career. Known informally as the "Clown Prince of Denmark," Borge received America's highest award in the arts, the Kennedy Center Honor.

A couple perform a folk dance in Solvang, California, in the Danish Days Festival held annually to celebrate Denmark's Constitution Day on June 5.

Danish Culture Today

Although these institutions have changed significantly during the 20th century, they continue to exert a presence as centers for contemporary Danish culture. Private colleges such as Grand View and Dana continue to support programs and classes on Scandinavian studies. Many Lutheran churches trace their history to Danish immigrant communities, and their congregations maintain Danish hymns, customs, and traditions during special occasions and especially during the Christmas season. Danish folk schools host programs to promote Danish history and culture. This type of cultural preservation is also evident in Danish American support for local museum and history centers, most notably the Danish Immigrant Museum in Elk Horn, Iowa.

Danish identity in America is expressed in subtle ways within private spheres, like telling stories and cooking Danish food in the home, as well as keeping holiday customs and practicing handiwork techniques such as embroidery or lacemaking. However, Americans' increased interest in ethnicity during the past two decades has increased the visibility of Danish culture. Visitors to the handful of Danish communities in America can attend ethnic festivals, sample Danish foods, hear Danish music, participate in Danish folk dances, and share in other public presentations of Danish culture.

Retaining Links with the Past

Whereas most of the early Danish immigrants worked as farmers, tradesmen, factory workers, and domestic maids, contemporary Danes have become so assimilated they are represented in every field and profession. Yet even second- and third-generation Danish Americans retain links to the land of their ancestors. They often stay in contact with relatives in Denmark and keep up to date about international news that concerns Denmark.

The progressive politics of Denmark are compatible with the sense of civic-mindedness and social conscience held by many Danish Americans. Danish liberalism, however, can contrast sharply with the strain of religious and social conservatism within Danish American culture, which is not clearly present in Denmark. This difference between Danes and Danish Americans is not a source of tension—rather, it leads to mutual curiosity and amusement.

See also

• Finns (Volume 4)
• Greenlanders (Volume 4)
• Mormons (Volume 7)
• Norwegians (Volume 8)
• Swedes (Volume 10)

The Dominican Republic occupies half of the island of Hispaniola in the Caribbean. The Dominican population in the United States is relatively new and one of the fastest growing of all immigrant groups, now second only to Mexicans.

The earliest migrants were largely professionals who started entering the United States in the early 1960s. Following the assassination of the dictator Rafael Trujillo in 1961, civil war, and a subsequent U.S. invasion in 1965, they were fleeing political repression. The next wave of migrants, in the late 1960s and early 1970s, were middle-class economic migrants. Since then the large numbers of Dominicans who have left (particularly in the 1980s and 1990s—around 250,000 and 234,000 respectively) have been economic migrants drawn from the lower-middle and working classes.

Those Dominicans who leave the Dominican Republic tend to have a better job and education level than those left behind, many of whom cannot afford the fare to leave. Dominican Americans live predominantly on the East Coast, particularly around New York City and New Jersey. In New York the Washington Heights and Queens areas are home to thousands of Dominicans, as are the New Jersey suburbs. There is also a substantial Dominican population in Florida around the Miami area. In addition to approximately 750,000 Dominicans who are legally resident in the United States, there are a large unspecified number of undocumented Dominicans.

Employment for Dominican Americans

Dominican Americans work in industries such as manufacturing, particularly in the garment industry in New York City, and in the hotel and restaurant service industries. In areas such as Manhattan some Dominican Americans run their own grocery and convenience stores, while others work in them.

Dominican American women tend to work outside the home much more in the United States than they would back in the Dominican Republic. Many women also work in the garment industry. Their increased financial independence has important consequences, since women tend to have more say in the running of the family than they would at home. Families also tend to be smaller than in the Dominican Republic.

Many Dominican migrants find themselves overqualified for the jobs they occupy in the United States although they earn more than they would at home for

> **Community organizations**
>
> Both political and nonpolitical organizations exist. The former include Concilio de Organizaciones Dominicanas (Council of Dominican Organizations), Associacion Nacional de Dominicanos Ausentes (National Association of Absent Dominicans), and Alianza Dominicana. The latter include sports, recreational, and educational associations.

Exhausted Dominican refugees, taken from a small sailing boat by a U.S. Coast Guard cutter off the Florida Keys, wait to be interviewed by immigration officials.

more skilled work. Often Dominican migrants move to the United States simply to earn enough money to save for a good lifestyle back on the island. While men may dream of returning, some women grow used to their financial independence and would prefer to stay in the United States.

Culture, Education, and Politics

In the home families speak Spanish, and newspapers such as *El Diario* and *El Tiempo* are aimed at Dominican American communities. A major source of entertainment for many is baseball. They avidly follow their home teams, and the game is considered almost a religion. Education remains important to Dominican Americans, who press their children to study hard and aim for a better economic future. In Washington Heights, New York City, some of the schools are predominantly Dominican, and parents have started to sit on school boards to shape their children's education. Increasingly the Dominican American population has become politicized, and associations lobby for citizenship rights, for undocumented workers, and against police violence following the police shooting of José Garcia in 1992. They also work to guarantee rights, such as the right to vote in national elections in the Dominican Republic.

Notable Dominican Americans
Mary Joe Fernandez (1971–), tennis player.
Oscar de la Renta (1932–), fashion designer.

See also
• Caribbean peoples (Volume 2)
• Cubans (Volume 3)
• Emigrés and refugees (Volume 4)
• Jamaicans (Volume 6)

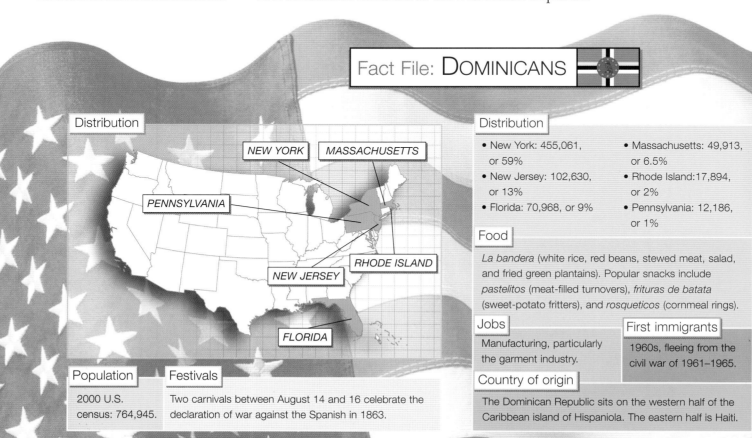

Fact File: DOMINICANS

Distribution

NEW YORK   MASSACHUSETTS

PENNSYLVANIA

RHODE ISLAND

NEW JERSEY

FLORIDA

Distribution

- New York: 455,061, or 59%
- New Jersey: 102,630, or 13%
- Florida: 70,968, or 9%
- Massachusetts: 49,913, or 6.5%
- Rhode Island:17,894, or 2%
- Pennsylvania: 12,186, or 1%

Food

La bandera (white rice, red beans, stewed meat, salad, and fried green plantains). Popular snacks include *pastelitos* (meat-filled turnovers), *frituras de batata* (sweet-potato fritters), and *rosqueticos* (cornmeal rings).

Jobs

Manufacturing, particularly the garment industry.

First immigrants

1960s, fleeing from the civil war of 1961–1965.

Country of origin

The Dominican Republic sits on the western half of the Caribbean island of Hispaniola. The eastern half is Haiti.

Population

2000 U.S. census: 764,945.

Festivals

Two carnivals between August 14 and 16 celebrate the declaration of war against the Spanish in 1863.

Dress and costume

History suggests that Western fashions and trends commonly have a profound effect on the cultures they encounter. Since they want to assimilate, ethnic migrants to North America often readily adopt Western attire. In contrast, there have been instances of forced assimilation in the past, such as when the U.S. government sometimes forced Native American tribal children to wear Western dress at state-run boarding schools. Whether worn voluntarily or by coercion, dress plays a vital role in keeping or recreating a cultural identity.

The vast majority of Americans utilize Western dress of trousers and skirts on a daily basis. Traditional ethnic dress is often adopted only for selected occasions, particularly religious observations and cultural celebrations. For example, Japanese women and men both in Japan and in the United States will often wear a kimono for an ethnically mixed formal occasion such as a wedding reception, where a Westerner might wear evening dress. Japanese may also wear the kimono for specifically Japanese religious observances at a Shinto shrine or Buddhist temple, or for a cultural activity such as the Japanese tea ceremony.

Traditional costume might also be worn to show affiliation or solidarity with one's own heritage, such as wearing tartan at a Highland games or green on St. Patrick's Day. In some cases Americans will adopt another culture's ethnic dress to show support or affiliation with that nationality, for example, a non-Indian woman might wear a sari to wed an Indian male.

Dress and Ethnicity

To show community feeling and ethnic continuity, people often wear ethnic dress in group situations. An example would be the use of the *tallit*, or prayer shawl, worn by Jewish boys during their *bar mitzvah*, celebrating entrance into manhood. This prayer shawl is identical to the one worn by all adult Jewish men, linking the boy to the men around him and to the community of faith at large, past and present.

Some groups within the United States continue to wear their traditional dress on a daily basis for a variety of reasons. First, traditional dress reinforces the values of the originating culture and the present people's association with their ancestors. Second, ethnic dress may be worn as a visual separation from the values or political agenda of Western culture. Primary examples of these ideas are found in the attire of religious group such as Mennonites, Amish, Hutterites, Muslims, and others.

Useful websites

The Costume Institute
(www.metmuseum.org/collections
/department.asp?dep=8)
Balch Institute for Ethnic Studies
(www.balchinstitute.org/
museum/rites/art.html)
The Customer's Manifesto
(www.costumes.org/pages/
fashiondress/traditiondress.htm)

Formal kimonos are worn at Oshogatsu, the Japanese New Year celebration. The long, flowing sleeves of the kimono to the left signify the woman wearing it is unmarried, while her older, married companions have shorter sleeves.

An Asian Indian woman shops for a salwar kameez *(a traditional garment) in the Indian district of Chicago, Illinois.*

Native American dress

The clothing of Native American peoples varied widely according to the climate, geography, and locally available materials in different regions, as well as to the differing lifestyles and cultures of tribes. Woven textiles were rarely made, and animals skins were widely used. They were tanned (a process in which unwanted skin and fur is removed) to create soft materials, which were sometimes dyed bright colors. The animal skins were often left unshaped, with paws and tails retained for decoration. Other decorations included embroideries made with porcupine quills and fringed edging. Typical garments included loincloths for men and short skirts for women. In warm regions an apron back and front was added, with cloaks or ponchos in bad weather. In cooler areas men wore a loose hip-length tunic and leggings, and women wore long dresses and leggings. In cold Arctic regions peoples like the Innuit wore clothing made from animal furs. The fur was worn on the inside of the garment, close to the body, and clothing was tailored to keep people as snug as possible. Both sexes wore hooded tunics or coats, trousers, and boots.

Religious Groups

The Mennonites and Amish are two sects of the Anabaptist faith established in the 17th century. There are about 100,000 observers of these faiths in 22 states, including about 45,000 in Ohio. Men usually dress in a plain suit, often in black, dark blue, or purple, and they wear a broad-brimmed hat. In the summer time the hat is made of straw. For the winter months a black felt hat is worn. Hair is cut in a "bowl style," and the men grow beards without mustaches. Men also wear trousers, suspenders, and high-laced shoes. Women wear plain dresses with long sleeves, a bonnet, and an apron. They wear a white prayer covering if married, a black prayer covering if they are single. A woman is usually married in a blue or purple dress, mid-calf length with no fancy trim. A woman will wear her wedding dress for Sunday service; and when she dies, it will be used for her burial. The Mennonites do not wear jewelry.

The Hutterites hold all property in common and believe community life is necessary for survival, peace, harmony, and freedom. Traditionally they farm as a community and tend to have a very religious lifestyle. Women wear a bonnet under a polka-dot handkerchief, an ankle-length skirt with matching apron, a colorful blouse, and a jacket that matches the skirt. Women are allowed to wear colorful fabrics as long as they maintain the traditional Hutterite dress and their strong religious beliefs. Hutterite men tend to wear a basic black suit with a white collared shirt.

A dress code that relies almost entirely on colorful fabrics is that of the Asian Indian community, which has inspired some of the most beautiful and lavish ethnic costumes in history. Today many Asian Indian women still wear either the graceful sari if they are Hindu or the practical *salwar kameez* if they are Muslim. Both can be made of bright cotton or silk, and they are usually embroidered. The *salwar kameez* comes with a coordinating scarf known as a "dupatta," which is used to cover the head.

Some Muslims from other countries also wear clothing that derives from their ethnic costume. Most notable are the garments worn by women to cover their faces, head, or hands. This custom is derived from the Islamic teaching about *hijab*, or modesty, which may be interpreted slightly differently in different countries. In some countries *hijab* means the entire body must be covered except the hands, face, and feet. For women in other countries, wearing a head scarf and long, robelike garments is considered enough for modesty. Some women also choose to cover their faces, either partially or entirely, with a veil. Muslim women do not universally observe *hijab* by covering, in whole or in part, their bodies.

Discrimination and Dress

The government of the United States has prohibited discrimination based on religion, national origin, race, color, or sex by the Civil Rights Act of 1964. Part of this act could also serve as a basis to prosecute any harassment or discrimination due to accent or dress associated with a particular religion, ethnicity, or country of origin. Employers, schools, unions, and others are required to "reasonably accommodate the religious practices of an employee or prospective employee, unless doing so would create an undue hardship."

The terrorist attacks of September 11, 2001, led to some harassment of Arab Americans and others. Often these hate crimes were perpetrated against people wearing ethnic dress. Due to the media attention surrounding Osama bin Laden and his terror organization, Al Qaeda, some Americans came to associate the wearing of turbans, beards, or Middle Eastern dress with terrorism. For example, Sikhs were harassed for wearing green turbans and beards. The United States government reminded employers and other Americans of the strict laws regarding toleration.

See also

- Amish (Volume 1)
- Asian Indians (Volume 1)
- Japanese (Volume 6)
- Jews (Volume 6)

Scottish Highland Games

Each year thousands of Americans take part in events like the Scottish Highland Games in Santa Rosa, California. Often participants dress in Scottish costume and compete in activities like piping, drumming, and country dancing. Here a bagpipe leader in full Highland dress, complete with sporran (purse), uses a baton to guide the marching pipers. Such festivals reinforce ethnic Scottish ties, and clan representatives, genealogists, and tartan sellers often attend.
For further information, *see*:
The Council of Scottish Clans and
   Associations
   (www.tartans.com/cosca/)
The Association of Scottish Games
   and Festivals (www.asgf.org/)

Dutch

Many familiar New York City areas take their names directly from the early Dutch influence. The Bowery takes its name from the Dutch word *bouwerie*, meaning "farm." The street after which the area is named once led to the farm of New Netherlands' governor Peter Stuyvesant. Staten Island takes its name from the States General, or "Staten-General" in Dutch, the legislative body that governed the Netherlands. The Dutch settlement of Nieuw Haarlem is today's Harlem. Wall Street is named after the wall around lower Manhattan built by the Dutch in a failed effort to keep the British from taking over their colony. Other modern cities with names of Dutch origin include New Holland, Pennsylvania, and Amsterdam, Ohio.

A 17th-century engraving of the natural harbor in New Amsterdam, where the Dutch sent colonists to settle from 1624.

The Dutch were among the first European settlers in North America, beginning with the exploration of the Hudson River by a Dutch vessel in 1609, just two years after the British had established a settlement in Virginia. Captain Henry Hudson of the Dutch East India Company sailed the *De Halve Maen* up the river in search of a shorter route to Asia and the East Indies. The Dutch settled a large portion of the eastern seaboard of the United States, from Connecticut to Pennsylvania, through the 1600s. Many well-known locations—Brooklyn, Harlem, Staten Island, Wall Street, and Coney Island—trace their names to this early Dutch influence. Today the influence of Dutch Americans far outweighs their relatively small numbers because of the important role they played in settling early America. People of Dutch ancestry make up a significant part of the Canadian population. Dutch settlers loyal to the British crown moved to Canada after the American Revolution (1775–1783); the next wave of settlers were farmers in the 19th century; while the most recent and largest influx of Dutch immigrants came in the 1950s.

Early Settlements

The Dutch dominated European commerce in the 1600s. The Dutch capital of Amsterdam was a world financial center managing a commercial empire with colonies in Asia, Africa, and the Americas. Dutch settlement of North America began in 1614, when the Dutch navigator Adriaen Block mapped the coast of Manhattan, and the Netherlands granted a trading charter to 13 Dutch businessmen. These first settlers established Fort Nassau on the Hudson River near present-day Albany, New York, making it the second-oldest European settlement in the United States. This outpost became the center of the developing fur trade. Within 10 years the Hudson River valley was known as the colony of New Netherlands. In 1624, 10 Dutch families arrived to establish a new settlement on the tip of present-day Manhattan Island, and the Dutch government encouraged more of its citizens to settle in the area known as New Amsterdam. In 1625 New Amsterdam became the capital of New Netherlands. A year later the governor of New Netherlands, Peter Minuit, made one of the most famous financial transactions in the history of North America when he purchased Manhattan Island from a local Native American tribe for the equivalent

Distribution

Based on an estimated 8 million living in the following regions:

- North–central states: 2.8 million, or 35%
- Southern states: 1.92 million, or 24%
- Western states: or 1.92 million, or 24%
- Northeastern states: 1.44 million, or 18%

Most populous states:

- New York
- Pennsylvania
- Michigan
- Florida
- Wisconsin
- Iowa
- Washington
- Ohio
- Illinois

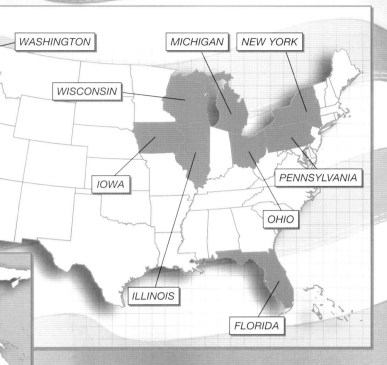

WASHINGTON · MICHIGAN · NEW YORK · WISCONSIN · IOWA · PENNSYLVANIA · OHIO · ILLINOIS · FLORIDA

Region of origin

Netherlands

The nation of the Dutch—the Netherlands—is one of the "Low Countries" on the northwest coast of Europe, along with Belgium and Luxembourg.

Population

U.S. census (2000): 8 million people of Dutch origin
Canadian census (1996): 916,215 people of Dutch origin

Religion

Many Dutch in the 19th century belonged to the Dutch Reformed Church (Protestant), but other religions were common, including Roman Catholics and Quakers. The jailing of some orthodox dissenters from the Dutch Reformed Church for holding unauthorized church services in the 19th century prompted them to emigrate to North America.

Jobs

In the early years most Dutch immigrants to the United States and Canada were farmers, but the immigrant population gradually moved toward more urban trades. By 1880 the furniture industry of Grand Rapids, Michigan, was largely Dutch-owned and staffed. Many urban Dutch opened shops that catered to Dutch clientele. By the mid-20th century Dutch Americans dominated the refuse collection business in Chicago. Today Dutch Americans work in all sectors of employment, from manufacturing and laboring, through technical, sales, and administrative occupations, to managerial jobs and the professions.

Dates of major arrivals

- 1882: The peak year of immigration to the U.S. from Holland, when a total of 359,000 Dutch arrived in the North America.
- 1951–53: The peak years of immigration to Canada, when an average of 20,000 immigrants arrived each year.

Community organizations

Holland Society of New York, founded 1855 (www.hollandsociety.com)
Netherlands Museum, Holland, Michigan, established 1937 (www.michmarkers.com/Pages/L0622.htm)
A.C. Van Raalte Institute, established 1994, Holland, Michigan (www.hope.edu/resources/vri)
Many local communities sponsor "Dutch Clubs."

Notable Dutch Americans

Three American presidents claim colonial Dutch ancestry: Martin Van Buren (1782–1862), Theodore Roosevelt (1858–1919), and Franklin D. Roosevelt (1882–1945).

Festivals

Tulip Festival, Holland, Michigan. Held annually in May and one of the largest U.S. tulip festivals (www.tuliptime.org).
Canadian Tulip Festival, Ottawa. Held annually in May since 1952, it is the world's largest tulip festival. It is a donation from the Dutch government in thanks for Canadian help during World War II. (www.tulipfestival.ca/).
Dutch American Heritage Day. Celebrated since 1991 on November 16 in honor of the day in 1776 that Dutch forces on the Caribbean island of St. Eustatius returned the salute of an American ship, making the Netherlands the first country to salute the flag of the newly independent United States.

The one-legged Dutch governor of New Amsterdam, Peter Stuyvesant, surrendering the settlement to the British, who renamed it New York.

Going Dutch

Dutch colonial: a style of architecture characterized by a gambrel roof with overhanging eves.

Dutch courage: courage that is artificially stimulated, especially by alcoholic drink.

Dutch treat: also to "go dutch," when each person pays his or her own way.

Dutch sauce or "Hollandaise" sauce: a rich sauce of butter, egg yolks, and lemon juice or vinegar.

of $24. The Dutch expanded their trading posts up and down the eastern seaboard, firmly establishing themselves in the Hudson and Delaware river valleys in present-day Connecticut, New Jersey, and Pennsylvania. In 1647 Peter Stuyvesant became governor of New Netherlands. Stuyvesant was a stern leader who was unpopular with the settlers, but the Dutch population of New Netherlands grew from 2,000 to 8,000 during his years in office. In 1664 the British fleet arrived off the coast of New Amsterdam, demanding the surrender of the Dutch colony. While Stuyvesant wanted to fight, lack of support from the Dutch settlers led him to surrender New Netherlands to the British. They renamed New Amsterdam "New York" after the king's brother, the duke of York.

Waves of Immigration

Three distinct phases of Dutch immigration are evident. The first came during the commercial expansion of the 17th century before the loss of New Netherlands to the British. Although the Dutch government supported the emigration of merchants to establish commercial ventures, most families were reluctant to leave Holland, fearful of the ocean passage, the wilderness of the new land, and tales of hostile Indians. As a result, many of the new settlers were unemployed laborers, agricultural tenants, and youths from orphanages and poorhouses whose passage was paid by the Dutch government. The loss of New Netherlands reduced Dutch immigration to a trickle.

The second phase of Dutch immigration occurred in the 19th century, a time when America appeared to offer better opportunities than were available in the Netherlands. Some Dutch immigrated in groups, including entire congregations led by their pastors or priests. In 1846 religious leader Albertus Van Raalte led more than 1,000 followers to a new settlement in western Michigan. Within two years more than 4,000 people lived in New Holland, as they called their new home. Another 900 immigrants followed Hendrik Pieter Scholte to central Iowa to found the community of Pella. Of Dutch emigrants in the 19th century, 90 percent went to the United States—more than 340,000 people between 1820 and 1900.

The third phase of Dutch immigration occurred in the 20th century, when years of war and economic depression strained the ability of the Netherlands to provide for its growing population. Between 1900 and 1950 the population of the Netherlands doubled, and the Dutch government began to encourage its citizens to emigrate to the United States and Canada. In 1949 the Dutch government even offered to pay the transportation costs for citizens willing to relocate. By this time the United States began to restrict immigration. The annual quota for Dutch immigrants was only 3,136 people. By the early 1950s more than 40,000 Dutch were on waiting lists to enter the United States. This restriction led the Dutch to emigrate to other areas: More than one million went to Canada, Australia, and other countries shortly after World War II. Between 1945 and 1965 only 80,000 Dutch came to the United States, representing only 19 percent of Dutch emigrants during the period. Another 35 percent went to Canada and 29 percent to Australia. Others chose New Zealand and South Africa. Since the United States repealed the national origins basis for immigration quotas in 1968, Dutch immigration has remained low, averaging fewer than 1,000 each year.

Cultural Life

The tendency of Dutch settlers to cluster into tightly bound communities has given the group greater visibility than its relatively small numbers warrant. The tradition of living in stable, like-minded communities has characterized Dutch immigrants to North America for hundreds of years. For example, United States census data show that in 1850, 75 percent of all Dutch emigrants to the United States lived in fewer than 1 percent of United States counties. United States census data for 2000 shows that the 8 million Americans of Dutch descent remain clustered in a few well-defined areas, including central and western New York, eastern and western Pennsylvania, central and southern Michigan, central Florida, eastern Wisconsin, central Iowa, central Washington, northeastern and southwestern Ohio, and central and northeastern Illinois. The tendency of the Dutch to cluster in what were originally rural areas reflects the background of those who came to America. Most arrived from rural villages and farms rather than the Dutch seaport cities and government centers. Fewer than 15 percent of 18th- and 19th-century emigrants were professionals or businessmen. Despite their meager beginnings, the industrious nature of the Dutch, along with traditional values stressing frugality and self-help, lifted them from poverty. The group's ethnic identity began to break down during World War I. The use of Dutch language aroused suspicions, and many uninformed Americans mistook the Dutch for Germans. After a Dutch church and school were burned near Pella, Iowa, the state governor ordered the use of English in all

Dutch Canadians

There was a surge in Dutch immigration to Canada in the 1950s and 1960s: From 1951 to 1953 an average 20,000 Dutch immigrants arrived each year. The increase was a result of U.S. immigration restrictions and a special relationship between Canada and the Netherlands. During World War II Canada provided a safe haven for Crown Princess Juliana of the Netherlands and Canadian troops played a key role in the liberation of the country from Nazi occupation. Dutch immigrants since the war have been skilled industrial workers, technicians, business people, and professionals.

A Dutch American marching band wearing the traditional "klompen," or wooden shoes, during a festival in Holland, Michigan.

The annual tulip festival in the Dutch-settled town of Holland, Michigan, is one of the biggest Dutch festivals of the year.

See also

- Belgians (Volume 1)
- Colonial America (Volume 3)
- Festivals (Volume 4)
- World War I (Volume 10)
- World War II (Volume 10)

public assembly areas. The Dutch language nearly vanished in the United States between the world wars. Only one of 25 Dutch-language newspapers printed in the United States in 1918 survived at the end of World War II. However, Dutch Americans continue to honor their heritage. The Netherlands Museum opened in Holland, Michigan, in 1937. Fifty years later the city of Holland created the Joint Archives of Holland to preserve the documentary history of this Dutch American community. In 1960 the citizens of Pella created a "historical village," with 21 buildings designed in traditional Dutch styles.

Links across the Ocean

The ties between Holland and the United States have always been strong, beginning with Dutch support for the colonists against the British in the Revolutionary War. Benjamin Franklin once wrote, "In love of liberty and in the defense of it, Holland has been our example." Since the establishment of formal diplomatic relations between the two countries in 1782 these ties have remained intact. John Adams served as the first United States envoy to the Netherlands and secured the first loan for the new Congress from three Amsterdam banks. Between 1780 and 1794 the Netherlands loaned the United States an amount equivalent to the new country's entire foreign debt. The support between the countries has never wavered. The Netherlands was one of the first countries to ally itself with the United States after the Japanese attack on Pearl Harbor in 1941. In return, the landings of the United States Army's 82nd and 101st Airborne Divisions in the occupied Netherlands in September 1944 opened the door for liberation from Nazi occupation.

The Dutch Today

Over the years the Dutch in North America have moved from predominantly rural areas to more urban settings, as Dutch farming communities gave way to professional occupations. This pattern is especially evident in the last half of the 20th century. In 1948 some 48 percent of Dutch emigrants to the United States were still farmers. Within 20 years the number had dropped to 1 percent, with most Dutch emigrants belonging to white-collar professions. Recent Dutch immigrants have settled in large metropolitan areas, including Los Angeles, New York City, and the suburbs of New Jersey in the United states, and Toronto and Vancouver in Canada. The traditional pockets of Dutch settlement in North America remain strong, exemplified by the explosive growth of Holland, Michigan, in the late 20th century, nearly doubling the area's population. Modern Dutch Americans hold fast to many traditions, including the springtime tulip festivals. The world's largest tulip festival, held in Ottawa, is a donation from the Dutch government in thanks for Canada's help during World War II.

East Africans

The geographical region of East Africa includes Somalia, Ethiopia, Djibouti, and Eritrea—also known as the Horn of Africa—as well as Kenya, Uganda, and Tanzania. Each country consists of several group divisions, some with distinct languages, dialects, and religions. East Africa saw much upheaval in the latter part of the 20th century, resulting in waves of emigration from the region.

The Horn of Africa

In recent years Somalia has experienced wars with Ethiopia, famines, droughts, and economic instabilities, all contributing to its political volatility. In the 1990s the United States and United Nations interceded to deliver humanitarian aid and assist in restoring order. Both organizations withdrew in the mid-1990s, and political problems persist. The Somalian population today is 9.7 million, mostly living in rural areas. The principal language is Somali, and the dominant religion is Sunni Muslim.

Ethiopia has been heavily involved in conflict since 1962, when it annexed neighboring Eritrea. The war continued for 30 years as Eritrea attempted to gain independence. In a 1993 internationally monitored referendum 99.8 percent of Eritreans voted for independence, although the borders were not defined clearly. After a brief peace war again resulted over a minor border dispute in May 1998 and over differences in ethnicity: Eritreans are predominantly Muslim, while in Ethiopia the dominant group is Coptic Christian. The May 1998–June 2000 war resulted in 100,000 deaths and diverted millions of dollars from much-needed development. At the end of May 2000 Ethiopia claimed to have ended the war with victory over Eritrea, while Eritrea claimed a tactical withdrawal. It is estimated that up to 750,000 Eritrean refugees fled their homes during the conflict.

The remaining country in the Horn of Africa, the small republic of Djibouti, is a former Italian, British, and French colony, independent since 1977. Its population consists of a Somali majority and is almost entirely Muslim.

Kenya, Tanzania, and Uganda

The republic of Kenya is bordered on the east by Somalia and the Indian Ocean, on the south by Tanzania, the west by Uganda, and the north by Sudan and Ethiopia. As a result of immigration the population consists of various ethnic African groups and today totals 28.2 million, 73 percent of whom live in rural

Swahili

Swahili is a language spoken by an estimated 50 million people and, after Arabic, is the most widely understood language in Africa. It is the official language of Tanzania and Kenya and is used extensively in Uganda, Somalia, and Ethiopia. Many speakers of Swahili speak two or more other languages and use Swahili as a common means of communication. Although English is still an important language in post-independence East Africa, Swahili plays an increasingly vital role in the daily commercial, political, cultural, and social life of the region at every level of society. Many East African immigrants to North America continue to speak Swahili in their homes and communities.

Children play in an area known as the "Green Line" in Mogadishu, the capital city of Somalia. In the 1990s the Green Line was the heavily disputed dividing line between the territories of northern and southern Somalian warlords.

Fact File: EAST AFRICANS

Distribution

Most populous states:
- New York
- California
- Texas

Most populous cities:
- New York, New York
- Los Angeles, California
- Washington, D.C.
- Atlanta, Georgia
- Houston, Texas

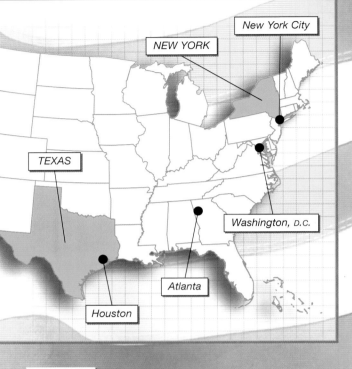

NEW YORK • New York City • CALIFORNIA • TEXAS • Los Angeles • Houston • Atlanta • Washington, D.C.

Region of origin

East Africa

The geographical region of East Africa includes Somalia, Ethiopia, Eritrea, Djibouti, Kenya, Uganda, and Tanzania.

Festivals

Kwanzaa (December 26 through January 1).
Juneteenth (June 18 and 19).

Community organizations

Institute for African American Studies (www.uga.edu/iaas)
The Kenyan Community Abroad (www.kenyansabroad.org/index.asp)
The Somali Resource and Heritage Center (Ottawa, Canada)
    (www.angelfire.com/ma3/somheritage/)
OATH (Organization of African Traditional Healers)
    (www.mamiwata.com/OATH.html)
National Association of Juneteenth Lineage
    (www.juneteenth.com/najl.htm)

Useful websites

Somalihome Online (www.somalihome.com/)
The Somali Resource and Heritage Center (Ottawa, Canada)
    (www.angelfire.com/ma3/somheritage/)
Kenya Hakuna Matata! (www.kenya.de/index.htm)
Ethiopia Online (www.ethiopiaonline.net)
African Online–Horn of Africa (www.africaonline.com/site/horn/)
East Africa Web Directory (http://dir.eastafricaweb.com/)
Africanet: Uganda (www.africanet.com/africanet/country/uganda)
The Official Kwanzaa Website (www.officialkwanzaawebsite.org)

Population

The 2000 U.S. census lists a total of 36.5 million African Americans, comprising 34.7 million black or African Americans and 1.8 million mixed (black combined with one or more races).

Jobs

East African immigrants run restaurants, grocery stores, tailors, and specialized hair salons.

Religion

East Africans practice many of the world's leading religions: Islam, Christianity (including a host of Coptic Christian churches), Buddhism, Hinduism, and Islam. Many people also follow traditional African belief systems.

Food

Traditional Kenyan dishes include *ugali* (cornmeal gruel), *m'chuzi wa kuku* (chicken with coconut), *samaki na nazi* (fish and coconut), *nyama na irio* (Kenyan beef and blended potatoes). Ethiopian dishes include *injera* (traditional bread), *iab* (cottage cheese and yogurt), *doro wat* (chicken stew), *sega wat* (lamb stew), and *dabo kolo* (fried cookies). In Djibouti the food is French-influenced and features local produce such as lentils, flat bread, chicken and fried meats, and Red Sea fish, baked or barbecued in a spicy sauce. In Tanzania thin pancakes called *chapati majis* are served as a cookie for dessert with tea or coffee. Other dishes include banana and meat stew with rice or potatoes. For dessert Tanzanian honey is often served with pineapple slices.

areas. Swahili and English are the main languages, with English used in business. One of the largest ethnic groups is the Bantu-speaking Kikuyu people who live in the highlands to the north of the capital, Nairobi. Religion in Kenya is diverse: 75 percent of the population are Christian, and 6 percent Muslim; the remainder follow indigenous beliefs.

Tanzania has a population estimated at 29 million, made up of various ethnic groups, including the Sukuma, Makonde, Chagga, Haya, and Nyamwezi. Major languages are Swahili and English. Most Tanzanians practice Christianity or Islam, and often combine these religions with local beliefs. To the north lies Uganda, a diverse mix of groups, with a population of 20 million. Uganda experienced many upheavals under the military dictatorship of Idi Amin (1969–1978). An unpredictable personality, Amin ordered the expulsion of Uganda's Asians in 1972, thrusting the nation into economic chaos. Amin, a Muslim, brutally suppressed other ethnic groups and political enemies, killing an estimated 200,000 during his regime. Tanzanian troops joined Ugandan nationalists to invade Uganda in 1978, and Amin was driven into exile in Libya.

Three slaves from Ethiopia, formerly Abyssinia, waiting in chains at a 19th-century slave market.

History of Immigration

It is difficult to establish the beginning of East African immigration into the United States, but it is thought that European settlers were taking Africans to the New World as slaves as early as the 1500s. The first clear documentation of involuntary African immigration to the United States dates to 1619. Totaling around 58,000 in the 1620s, the largest numbers of slaves lived in Virginia, South Carolina, and Pennsylvania. At the outbreak of the revolution in 1775 there were 500,000 slaves in the country, a figure that rose to 697,897 in 1790. By the time slavery was abolished in 1865, there were thought to be a total of 1.2 million slaves in the United States. Most of this number were taken from the west coast of Africa, but it is estimated that up to 100,000 came via the "Swahili Coast," an 1,800-mile stretch of Kenyan and Tanzanian coastline. This had been the site of cultural and commercial exchange between East Africa and the outside world since at least the second century A.D. The slave trade on the East African coast had existed for centuries, but it intensified during the early 19th century. Tippu Tip, one of the most powerful slave traders in Central and East Africa during that time, would raid villages in the

Education

For most East African immigrants education is very important. Children may live with extended families in order to attend school, and other sacrifices are made as necessary in order to obtain an education. The view is that education leads to self-empowerment, improves status within the social structure, and is a significant means for personal advancement. Most East African students concentrate their studies in the hard and social sciences, with some participation in the humanities.

A girl from the Masai tribe, originally from the Masai Mara, Kenya, wearing a traditional Masai robe, neck collar, and jewelry.

region and sell the captives to American and European merchants at the Zanzibar slave market. By the late 19th century the slave trade had all but ended, and the Swahili Coast returned to the export of spices.

After the abolition of slavery in 1865 African emigration to North America dropped—only 350 Africans arrived between 1891 and 1900. This changed between 1900 and 1950, when some 31,000 Africans immigrated voluntarily.

East African Emigration

East Africans emigrate to the United States for several reasons—to pursue university education; to reunite with established family members; to seek economic opportunities not available in Africa; and to escape from political instability. In recent years it has become possible to delineate the divisions of African immigrants in the United States. For example, the 2000 U.S. census reports that Ethiopians make up 13 percent of the African immigrant population.

East Africans enter the United States through New York, Los Angeles, Dallas, San Francisco, and Houston, and many continue to reside in these cities, developing significant communities. Their occupations range from street merchants and taxicab drivers to storekeepers. However, in some cases lack of education and limited job skills can mean that East African immigrants are open to exploitation by employers. Individuals may have to take low-paying jobs before progressing to higher-paying occupations.

Lifestyle and Culture

East African immigrants work to retain their cultures and customs while in the United States since most want to share their origins with the younger generations. Some East Africans have established camps and weekend schools to cultivate and develop their cultural identities and to teach East African traditions to their children. Family kinship is a very important aspect of East African societies. Families view different generations as parts of a complete unit in which the young care for the old, and senior family members impart wisdom and knowledge to the young. In addition, most East Africans have continuing bonds with relatives in their homelands.

Restaurants and grocery stores are major businesses in East African immigrant societies. In addition to selling East African foods they may incorporate other small concerns involving traditional skills such as tailoring or hair braiding. These stores also serve as informal cultural and community centers, providing places for people to meet, to form networks, and to keep their African heritage alive.

See also

- African Americans (Volume 1)
- African Canadians (Volume 1)
- Central Africans (Volume 2)
- Ethiopians (Volume 4)
- Liberians (Volume 6)
- Nigerians (Volume 8)
- North Africans (Volume 8)
- Slavery (Volume 9)
- South Africans (Volume 10)
- Southern Africans (Volume 10)
- West Africans (Volume 10)

Ecuador in South America is a small country of some 13 million people. The earliest migrants to the United States arrived in the 1960s as a result of two things: The 1965 change in U.S. immigration law, which allowed more Latin Americans to enter; and an alteration, in 1964, to the land law in Ecuador. This last led many peasants to move, first to cities in Ecuador, including the capital Quito, and then abroad when they were unable to maintain land the government had given them. The numbers of migrants has increased dramatically in recent years. With the collapse of the Ecuadorean economy in 1997, firms closed, jobs were lost, and the currency was devalued. As a result, in 1999 and 2000 it is estimated that one million Ecuadoreans left for the United States, Spain, and Italy. Currently, in addition to those Ecuadoreans who join relatives in the United States, or who enter by other legal means, estimates suggest there are half a million who are illegal immigrants.

Ecuadoreans and Assimilation

Ecuadorean Americans live predominantly on the East Coast, with the vast majority in the urban centers of New York City and New Jersey. New York has an established Ecuadorean community based largely in Queens and the Bronx. Roosevelt Avenue in Jackson Heights, Queens, has many Ecuadorean businesses, including travel agents and restaurants. The community is sufficiently established to allow newly arrived Ecuadoreans to move straight to the city. Smaller communities exist in Los Angeles, Chicago, and Miami. The immigrants interact not only with other Ecuadoreans but with other Hispanic groups. Most view their stay as temporary and plan to return home.

How Ecuadorean Americans make a living in the United States depends on which ethnic group they belong to, their economic level, and whether they are legal immigrants. Most Ecuadorean Americans send money back home. In 2000 Ecuadoreans abroad, including in the United States, sent back $1.2 billion, a sum second only to the country's oil revenue.

Spanish-speaking Ecuadoreans tend to live in Spanish-speaking enclaves and work in Hispanic environments or in menial jobs which do not rely on proficiency in English. They shop in Hispanic stores, watch Hispanic television, and read Spanish newspapers such as New York's *El Diario*. Some Ecuadoreans even absorb other Latino culture, such as the 15th birthday celebrations (*quinceaño*) for girls practiced by Mexican Americans.

A woman in Otavalo, Ecuador, fries a large pan of potatoes for sale in an open-air market.

The small numbers of Ecuadoreans of Indian origin, particularly those from Otavalo, Ecuador, who live in New York, are successful business people. They sell traditional woven goods and use their income to educate their children. They have learned Spanish and English as well as their native Quichua. The Indian Ecuadorean families are usually less patriarchal than those with Spanish roots.

Ecuadorean illegal immigrants work in restaurants and menial jobs that pay cash. They are more likely not to learn English and do not have access to welfare aid.

Arts and Culture

Music, particularly pan-pipe music, is very popular with Ecuadorean Americans. Ecuadorean music as a whole reflects the multiethnic and multicultural nature of the home country and incorporates many influences from African rhythms to traditional Andean forms.

Ecuadorean immigrants to North America are keen soccer fans and follow their national team on cable television. Tennis is also popular, and players such as Francisco Segura and Andres Gomez are national heroes. Ecuadorean foods include *llapingachos* (pancakes with mashed potato and cheese) and *caldo de pates*, a soup made from cattle hooves. *Paico* is a traditional drink made with fresh lemons.

See also

- Argentines (Volume 1)
- Chileans (Volume 2)
- Hispanic Americans (Volume 5)
- Paraguyans (Volume 8)
- Peruvians (Volume 8)

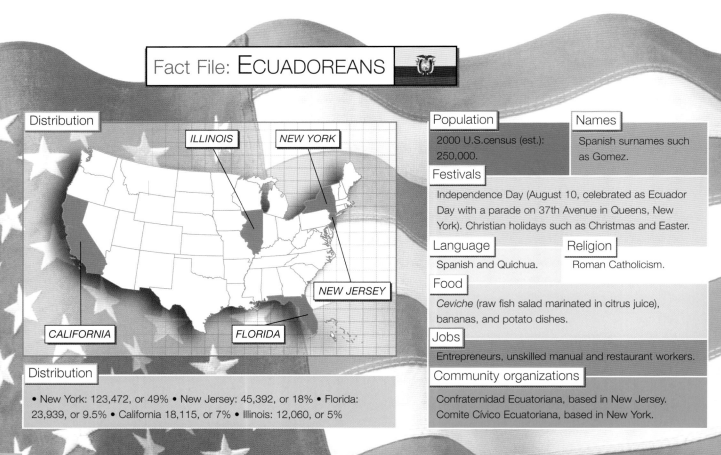

Fact File: ECUADOREANS

Distribution

ILLINOIS
NEW YORK
NEW JERSEY
CALIFORNIA
FLORIDA

Population

2000 U.S.census (est.): 250,000.

Names

Spanish surnames such as Gomez.

Festivals

Independence Day (August 10, celebrated as Ecuador Day with a parade on 37th Avenue in Queens, New York). Christian holidays such as Christmas and Easter.

Language

Spanish and Quichua.

Religion

Roman Catholicism.

Food

Ceviche (raw fish salad marinated in citrus juice), bananas, and potato dishes.

Jobs

Entrepreneurs, unskilled manual and restaurant workers.

Distribution

- New York: 123,472, or 49% • New Jersey: 45,392, or 18% • Florida: 23,939, or 9.5% • California 18,115, or 7% • Illinois: 12,060, or 5%

Community organizations

Confraternidad Ecuatoriana, based in New Jersey.
Comite Cívico Ecuatoriana, based in New York.

Education

Education was a part of the earliest American history. Puritans in New England offered free schooling for all children in the early 17th century. In 1635, only 15 years after their arrival in Massachusetts, the English immigrants organized the Roxbury Latin School. The first American college, Harvard, opened a year later. In the Middle Colonies there was more interest in practical education than there was in Puritan New England. Many different churches operated schools. The southern colonies did not have a tradition of public education and did not create state-supported schools until after the Civil War.

Early Colleges of Education

Harvard University, founded in 1636, is the oldest institution of higher education in the United States. Other colleges, including Bowdoin, Dartmouth, and Yale, soon followed, many begun by religious denominations. Colleges were more like theological schools than liberal arts colleges. The president of a college was always a clergyman, and professors and students alike were required to attend chapel daily. Almost anyone could "found" a college. Charters were easy to obtain, and colleges in the early national period were small.

Classical studies—mathematics, philosophy, Latin, and Greek—dominated early colleges. When the United States gained independence after the American Revolution (1775–1783), a "parallel program" including modern languages, sciences, political economy, and mathematics gained acceptance. Until about 1875 most immigrants came from northern and western Europe. These early colleges in the eastern United States largely reflect the English, Scots, French, and Dutch heritage of their founders. Colleges in the Midwest, such as St. Olaf College in Minnesota, founded in 1874, exemplified their founders' Scandinavian ancestry and Lutheran religious affiliation. From 1875 until about 1920 southern and eastern European immigrants dominated. They were more likely to attend existing institutions than create their own colleges and schools. Catholic parishes in strong ethnic communities in many cities had their own parochial schools.

In the later part of the 20th century immigrants from Latin America, the Caribbean, and Asia were the most numerous. Like the Greeks, Jews, Poles, and others before them, many of the new communities formed their own ethnic-based schools either in place of or as an addition to the public schools.

Catholic education

A large number of Catholic immigrants—many of whom were Irish—came to North America in the 19th century and began to set up their own educational institutions. One of the best known is the University of Notre Dame, Indiana, which was founded in 1842 by the Congregation of the Holy Cross, a French religious community. Originally it included a men's college, an elementary school, a college-preparatory school, a vocational school, and a novitiate. Catholics went on to establish many schools and colleges as an alternative to the system of secular public education in North America.

Harvard University is the oldest institution of higher learning in the United States. Founded in 1636 by English colonists to reflect English education, the university has grown from nine students with a single master to an enrollment of 18,000 degree candidates today.

More than 20 million American adults receive some form of education. Some participate in traditional courses, others in discussion groups, seminars, reading programs, correspondence courses, and more recently, online learning. Some adults are completing an unfinished education. Others want to improve themselves personally or improve their job qualifications. The tradition is strong in America. Benjamin Franklin started one early adult program, and the government sent many adults to school during the 1930s Great Depression to be retrained and later made it possible for returning World War II soldiers to get an education.

The Morrill Act of 1862, also known as the Land Grant College Act, stimulated the growth of state colleges. The original purpose of the grant was to establish state institutions to educate people in agriculture, home economics, and the mechanical arts.

The first state-funded school to educate teachers began in 1839 in Massachusetts. Teaching was not thought to be appropriate for the upper classes, who were more likely to receive a classical education and pursue other professions. "Normal" schools arose out of a desire to improve public schools by training teachers. Most schools met only four months a year, attendance was erratic, and teachers often were untrained. Normal schools stressed practical, everyday learning and provided future teachers with laboratory classrooms in which to learn their profession. As public education grew more formal, normal schools evolved into teachers' colleges that awarded bachelor of education degrees.

Ethnic Education

W.E.B. DuBois and Booker T. Washington both helped shape African American education after the Civil War (1861–1865). Although allies early in their careers, their views later diverged. Washington, who headed Tuskegee Institute, taught newly freed African Americans to be teachers, craftsmen, and businessmen, so that they could live productive lives. He emphasized learning by going over theories and abstract ideas. DuBois felt the "talented tenth" of the African American population should be able to be more than farmers and "money-makers." He hoped to develop the leaders of the race through a classical college education.

Washington's Tuskegee was one of dozens of institutes founded after the Civil War to educate newly freed slaves. Many grew into accredited higher educational institutions. Howard University and Hampton University are among 107 historically black colleges and universities remaining. After the Civil War many Southern states tried to limit the education of former slaves, who were forbidden in some states even to learn to read. What schools existed were segregated into black schools, Indian schools, and white schools. The U.S. Supreme Court ratified the concept of "separate but equal" facilities in its 1899 case *Plessy v. Ferguson*.

This principle was overturned in the Supreme Court decision *Brown v. Board of Education* in 1954. In 1950 a black seven-year-old, Linda Carol Brown, had tried to attend a white school in Kansas but was refused entry. Her parents protested, and the Supreme Court agreed, saying, "Separate educational facilities are inherently unequal." Desegregation followed over the next decade.

Sketch showing a 19th-century school for black children at the Freedmen's Bureau in Richmond, Virginia. The bureau was established at the end of the Civil War to provide humanitarian aid, legal protection, and education, mainly—but not exclusively—for ex-slaves and their children.

Native American Education

In what is now regarded as a misguided government policy, many Native American youths were taken from their homes in the late 19th century and transported thousands of miles to "Indian schools." While the intent was benign—to "civilize" rather than to subjugate—children were forced to cut their hair, wear Western clothes, speak English, and adopt an entirely foreign culture and way of life. Many died on the journey and still more from exposure to new diseases. Those who survived often found themselves unwelcome in white society despite their painful acculturation. Many who returned to their tribes were no longer accepted there either. The Carlisle Indian Industrial School in Pennsylvania was one of the most famous, or notorious, of these schools. It opened in 1879 and over the next 39 years hosted students from nearly every Native American tribe—its most famous pupil was Jim Thorpe, one of America's greatest sportsmen.

Not all Indian schools were such disasters. The Red Cloud Indian School was founded in 1888 at the request of Chief Red Cloud of the Oglala Sioux tribe at the Pine Ridge Reservation in South Dakota. It and others like it were supervised by tribal elders. The U.S. Congress created the Theodore Roosevelt School in northeastern Arizona in 1923 for Navajo children and, later, Apaches. In the mid-1800s the Choctaw and Cherokee Nations in what is now Oklahoma began an intensive education program for their children. Distances required boarding schools, but the tribes monitored the schools closely. Today the federal Bureau of Indian Affairs supervises nearly 200 tribal schools. There are also several dozen tribal colleges and community (two-year) colleges, such as the Turtle Mountain Community College on the reservation of the Turtle Mountain Ojibwa in North Dakota.

Private and Home Schools

Thousands of private schools exist at every level of education. Religious institutions, such as Catholic or Hebrew schools, ground their students in the beliefs and traditions of their respective faiths. Other schools, such as Arab American or Chinese American schools, are rooted in a common culture and language. Still other schools, such as Montessori schools, are based on pioneering educational principles. Private schools must meet basic state requirements concerning curriculum, safety, and the like. Since the 1980s more parents have chosen to educate their children at home. Most states now permit home schooling and provide curricula, supervision, and athletic activities to home-schooled children. In 2000 Patrick Henry College in Virginia was opened specifically for these young people.

A science class at the Carlisle Indian Industrial School, Pennsylvania, in 1915. The school was one of many that sought to assimilate Native American children into mainstream U.S. society.

Science and Technology

Colleges of higher education originally centered around teaching theology, but as education became increasingly secular in the 19th century some colleges reevaluated the subjects they taught. One result of this was the emergence of colleges specializing in science and technology. Two of the most influential were the Massachusetts Institute of Technology (MIT), founded in 1861, and the California Institute of Technology (CalTech), founded in 1891.

See also

- Assimilation (Volume 1)
- Immigrant experience (Volume 5)
- Literacy (Volume 6)
- Religion (Volume 9)

Egyptians

Egyptians have been in North America as a community for only a few decades. They are well assimilated into mainstream American life, but maintaining their own culture and heritage remains important to them. Canada's multicultural integration policies allow Egyptian Canadians to assimilate successfully into society while encouraging their cultural differences.

Waves of Immigration

Egyptians began emigrating in small numbers during the 1950s, mainly escaping the political upheaval of Egypt's struggle to overthrow the last monarch, King Farouk, and end European domination. The 1952 revolution, the nationalization policies of then-president Gamal Abdel Nasser, the defeat in the 1967 Arab–Israeli War, and economic instability all resulted in peak numbers of new immigrants in the 1960s and 1970s. The peak coincided with a change in the immigration policies of the United States under President John F. Kennedy, which removed the quota system allowing increased Egyptian immigration. Immigration reached its height in the 1970s; an estimated 85 percent of immigrants arrived in this period. These early immigrants came as professionals, skilled workers, and students. Most came with enough money to support themselves or had the education needed to be able to work in well-paid employment.

In the late 1980s and 1990s a large number of Egyptians came as investors and businessmen from the Gulf countries where they had been working for many years. Direct immigration from Egypt also continues from among educated professionals and well-off families.

Changing Lifestyles

The first wave of immigrants to North America was predominantly Christian, and the first Coptic church of Saint Mark was established in Toronto, Canada, in 1964. Today there are 64 parishes (51 in the United States and 13 in Canada). The church has always been a vital source of diverse social and employment services for Coptic immigrants, as well as the community at large. More recent waves of immigrants are predominantly Muslim.

Egyptian Americans are highly represented in the medical, research, educational, and technical professions, as well as in business. There is a high emphasis on education and a strong belief in its value. Thus 60 percent of Egyptian Americans and 90 percent of Egyptian Canadians hold a bachelor degree, and 50 percent hold a masters or doctorate degree.

Egyptians are mainly hard working, law-abiding citizens. Welfare recipients are very few, and the crime rate is among the lowest of any ethnic group. Most Egyptians fall within the middle and upper classes and have above average incomes.

Omar Sharif

Born Michel Shahoub in Alexandria, Egypt, in 1932, Sharif was the son of a successful timber merchant. He attended private English schools in Egypt. He converted from Christianity to Islam, changed his name to Omar Sharif, and became a movie star. He married and divorced actress Faten Hamamaand and has one son, Tarek. His most famous roles have included Sherif Ali ibn el Kharish in *Lawrence of Arabia* (1962) and the title role in *Dr. Zhivago* (1965). He also starred opposite American actress Barbra Streisand in *Funny Girl* (1968). Sharif's main passion is bridge, and he is a world-class player with an international tournament named in his honor. After more than 30 years in self-imposed exile Sharif returned to Cairo to live in 1996.

Cultural Life

The shape and intensity of identity varies widely between the different generations. For all generations ethnic affinity resides in food, extended-family rituals, and religious fellowships. Community centers and organizations often arrange social gatherings, Arabic language classes, and history classes to teach children about their homeland and culture. There are also community newspapers and magazines—for example, the *El Masri* and *El Mahroussa* newspapers published in Montreal. Traditional foods are consumed on a regular basis, particularly during the holy month of Ramadan, with close-knit family and friends gathering every day to break their fast. Many Egyptians enjoy congregating in the large number of Egyptian restaurants and cafés where traditional dishes are served. Diners can also enjoy smoking the *shisha* (hubble-bubble pipe), belly-dancing shows, and Egyptian-Arabic music.

Despite Egypt's pivotal role in maintaining peace in the Middle East, political involvement is minimal for Egyptian Americans, and lobbying for special causes is rare. However, Egyptians are very much concerned with their homeland and maintain ties with family through regular visits. Many Egyptians describe themselves as constantly "homesick," indicating their love for their ancestral home.

First immigrants

Even though a few Egyptians did arrive in North America in the early 1900s, it was on an individual basis, and exact numbers remain unknown. The date recognized as the major turning point or beginning of the process is 1964. The earliest of the immigrants were highly educated and well-off Egyptians considered the elite in their country. The majority of the early migrants were Christian.

See also

- Arab Americans (Volume 1)
- Assimilation (Volume 1)
- North Africans (Volume 8)
- Religion (Volume 9)

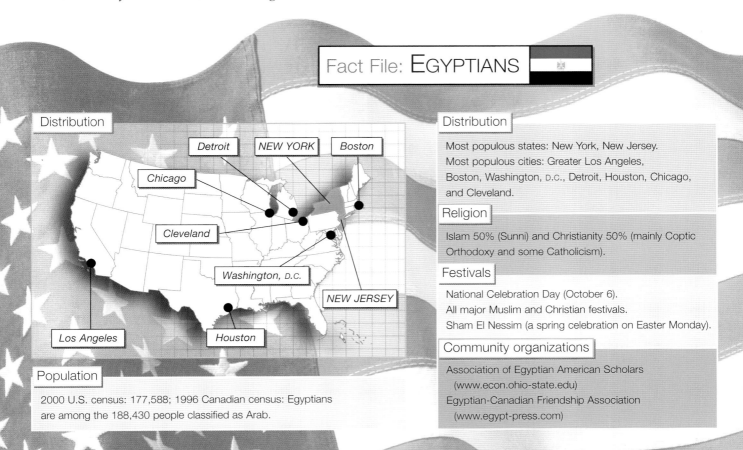

Fact File: EGYPTIANS

Distribution

Distribution

Most populous states: New York, New Jersey.
Most populous cities: Greater Los Angeles, Boston, Washington, D.C., Detroit, Houston, Chicago, and Cleveland.

Religion

Islam 50% (Sunni) and Christianity 50% (mainly Coptic Orthodoxy and some Catholicism).

Festivals

National Celebration Day (October 6).
All major Muslim and Christian festivals.
Sham El Nessim (a spring celebration on Easter Monday).

Community organizations

Association of Egyptian American Scholars
(www.econ.ohio-state.edu)
Egyptian-Canadian Friendship Association
(www.egypt-press.com)

Population

2000 U.S. census: 177,588; 1996 Canadian census: Egyptians are among the 188,430 people classified as Arab.

Map labels: Detroit, NEW YORK, Boston, Chicago, Cleveland, Washington, D.C., NEW JERSEY, Los Angeles, Houston

affirmative action government programs to provide equal opportunities to minority groups.

alien a foreign-born resident who has not been naturalized and is still a subject or citizen of another country.

assimilation the process by which an individual or a minority group adopts the values and practices of the dominant culture and loses its own cultural distinctiveness.

asylum the legal status granted to a foreign individual who fears political persecution if he or she is forced to return home.

bilingualism the ability to speak fluently in two languages.

census a comprehensive survey of a population designed to gather basic demographic information. In the United States the census is carried out every 10 years.

citizen a native or foreign-born member of a country who has legal and political rights within that country.

colony a territory ruled by another country.

cultural mingling a process that occurs when two or more cultures come into contact and interact with one another.

cultural retention the process by which an immigrant group or individual retains elements of their native heritage in a new society.

deportation the legal removal of an immigrant from a country.

diaspora the historical dispersal of a group of people of similar origins from their homeland to many lands.

discrimination the unfair denial of equal rights or opportunities to a group or individual based on cultural, social, or racial differences.

emigrant a person who leaves his or her homeland to live in a foreign country.

emigration the movement of people from their homeland to another country.

emigré a person forced to emigrate for political reasons.

ethnic group a group sharing common origins and cultural similarities, such as beliefs, values, customs, and language, geography, kinship, or race.

ethnicity identification with and inclusion within an ethnic group.

exclusion act a law passed to refuse entry into the United States to a certain race or nationality.

ghetto an often deprived urban area occupied predominantly by members of a single race or ethnic group.

immigrant a person who moves to a country other than his or her homeland.

immigration the settlement of people in a country other than that in which they were born.

indigenous a term referring to the original inhabitants of a land or territory.

integration the mixing of different racial groups within a community.

melting pot a phrase coined by Jewish playwright Israel Zangwill to refer to America's multicultural society in the early 20th century.

middle class a socioeconomic class broadly defined as those with middle income working in mental rather than manual occupations.

migrant a term describing someone who regularly moves from one place to another, often for economic reasons.

migration the movement of people from one country to settle in another.

minority group a subgroup of society characterized by factors including race, religion, nationality, gender, or culture.

multiethnic a term meaning belonging not to one single racial or ethnic group but to two or more.

multiculturalism a positive attitude toward cultural diversity that supports the right of ethnic groups to maintain their cultural distinctiveness within the dominant culture.

nativism an anti-immigrant U.S. political tradition, popular in the 19th century, that valued "real" Americans and their attitudes over more recent immigrants.

naturalization the legal process by which a foreign person becomes a citizen of a country with the same rights as a native-born citizen.

pluralism the equal coexistence of diverse ethnic groups within a single society.

prejudice the holding of unfounded ideas about groups or individuals based on negative stereotypes.

quota (system) a limit on the number of immigrants from particular countries allowed into another.

race the classification of people based on genetic characteristics or common nationality, history, or experiences.

racism discrimination against others based on an assumption of one's own racial superiority.

refugee a term referring to a person who lives in a foreign country to escape persecution at home.

repatriation the forcible or voluntary return of immigrants to their country of origin.

segregation the discriminatory separation or isolation of ethnic, social, or religious groups, for example, in restricted areas such as ghettos.

slavery the ownership of human beings by others.

social mobility the movement of groups or individuals within the social hierachy.

stereotype a usually negative categorization of all individuals within a group based on a rigid and inflexible image of the characteristics of that group.

upper class the more affluent members of society, especially those who have great wealth or hold an esteemed position in society.

urban renewal the rebuilding of deteriorating city neighborhoods, often those that have become ghettos.

working class a social group made up broadly of people in manual occupations.

Ansari, Maboud. *The Making of the Iranian Community in America.* New York: Pardis Press, 1993.

Avery, Donald. *Reluctant Host: Canada's Response to Immigrant Workers 1896–1994.* Toronto: McClelland & Stewart, 1995.

Axtell, James. *Natives and Newcomers: The Cultural Origins of North America.* New York: Oxford University Press, 2000.

Barry, Brian M. *Culture and Equality: An Egalitarian Critique of Multiculturalism.* Cambridge, MA: Harvard University Press, 2001.

Bodnar, John. *The Transplanted: A History of Immigrants in Urban America (Interdisciplinary Studies in History).* Bloomington, IN: Indiana University Press, 1987.

Brown, Dee Alexander. *Bury My Heart at Wounded Knee: An Indian History of the American West.* New York: Henry Holt and Company, 2001 revised edition.

Capp, Diana White Horse. *Brother against Brother: America's New War over Land Rights.* Bellevue, WA: Merril Press, 2002.

Chavez, Leo R. *Shadowed Lives: Undocumented Immigrants in American Society.* Belmont, CA: Wadsworth Pub, 1997.

Ciongoli, A. Kenneth, and Jay Parini. *Passage to Liberty: The Story of Italian Immigration and the Rebirth of America.* New York: Regan Books, HarperCollins, 2002.

Connell-Szasz, Margaret (ed.). *Between Indian and White Worlds: The Cultural Broker.* Norman, OK: University of Oklahoma Press, 1994.

Daniel Tatum, Beverly. *Assimilation Blues: Black Families in a White Community.* Boulder, CO: Basic Books, 2000.

Dezell, Maureen. *Irish America: Coming into Clover.* New York: Doubleday, 2001.

Diner, Hasia R. *Jewish Americans: The Immigrant Experience.* Southport, CT: Hugh Lauter Levin Assoc., 2002.

Do, Hien Duc. *The Vietnamese Americans.* Westport, CT: Greenwood Press, 2000.

Flores, Juan. *Divided Borders: Essays on Puerto Rican Identity.* Houston, TX: Arte Publico Press, 1993.

Franklin, John Hope, and Alfred A. Moss. *From Slavery to Freedom: A History of African Americans.* New York: Alfred A. Knopf, 2000.

Frye Jacobson, Matthew. *Whiteness of a Different Color: European Immigrants and the Alchemy of Race.* Cambridge, MA: Harvard University Press, 1999.

Getis, Arthur, Judith Getis, and I. E. Quastler (eds.). *The United States and Canada: The Land and the People.* New York: McGraw-Hill, 2000.

Gonzalez, Juan. *Harvest of Empire: A History of Latinos in America.* New York: Viking Press, 2000.

Gonzalez-Pando, Miguel. *The Cuban Americans.* Westport, CT: Greenwood Press, 1998.

Govorchin, Gerald Gilbert. *From Russia to America with Love: A Study of the Russian Immigrants in the United States.* Pittsburgh, PA: Dorrance Publishing, 1993.

Grimes, Kimberly M. *Crossing Borders: Changing Social Identities in Southern Mexico.* Tucson, AZ: University of Arizona Press, 1998.

Hegi, Ursula. *Tearing the Silence: Being German in America.* New York: Simon & Schuster, 1997.

Hilfiker, David. *Urban Injustice: How Ghettos Happen.* New York: Seven Stories Press, 2002.

Horn, Michiel. *Becoming Canadian: Memoirs of an Invisible Immigrant.* Toronto: University of Toronto Press, 1997.

Inada, Lawson Fusao (ed.). *Only What We Could Carry: The Japanese American Internment Experience.* Berkeley, CA: Heyday Books, 2000.

Kelley, Ninette, and Michael J. Trebilcock. *The Making of the Mosaic: The History of Canadian Immigration Policy.* Toronto: University of Toronto Press, 1998.

Kelly, Paul. *Multiculturalism Reconsidered: Culture and Equality and Its Critics.* Cambridge, England: Polity Press, 2003.

Kibria, Nazli. *Becoming Asian American: Second-Generation Chinese and Korean American Identities.* Baltimore, MD: Johns Hopkins University Press, 2002.

Lehman, Jeffrey (ed.). *Gale Encyclopedia of Multicultural America.* Detroit, MI: Gale Research, Inc., 2000.

Miscevic, Dusanka, and Peter Kwong. *Chinese Americans: The Immigrant Experience.* Southport, CT: Hugh Lauter Levin Assoc., 2000.

Morton Coan, Peter. *Ellis Island Interviews: In Their Own Words.* New York: Facts on File, 1997.

Naff, Alixa. *The Arab Americans.* Broomall, PA: Chelsea House, 1998.

Portes, Alejandro, and Rubén G. Rumbaut (eds.). *Ethnicities: Children of Immigrants in America.* Los Angeles, CA: University of California Press, 2001.

Stoffman, Daniel. *Who Gets In: What's Wrong with Canada's Immigration Program—And How to Fix It.* Toronto: Macfarlane Walter & Ross, 2002.

Takaki, Ronald. *Strangers from a Different Shore: A History of Asian Americans.* New York: Back Bay Books, 1998.

Thernstrom, Stephan A., Ann Orlov, and Oscar Handlin (eds.). *Harvard Encyclopedia of American Ethnic Groups.* Cambridge, MA: Belknap Press, 1980.

Waldinger, Roger (ed.). *Strangers at the Gates: New Immigrants in Urban America.* Los Angeles, CA: University of California Press, 2001.

Winks, Robin W. *The Blacks in Canada: A History.* Montreal: McGill-Queens University Press, 1997.

Relevant websites are listed separately with each entry.

1492 Christopher Columbus sails to North America

1534 Jacques Cartier sails up the St. Lawrence River

1535 Spain establishes colonial government in Mexico

1607 Settlers from England establish a colony in Jamestown, Virginia

1776 Declaration of Independence

1795 Naturalization Act restricts U.S. citizenship to "free white males" who reside in the United States for five years

1798 Alien and Sedition Act allows deportation of "dangerous" foreigners. Naturalization Act increases the residency requirement to 14 years

1802 Congress reduces residency requirement from 14 years to four

1808 Congress bans importation of slaves

1819 Steerage Acts: data collected on immigration for the first time

1820 Chinese arrive in California

1830 Indian Removal Act forces Native Americans to give up their lands east of the Mississippi River

1834 Slavery abolished in British North America (Canada)

1840s Major immigration of Irish and Germans due to crop failures

1846 Mexican–American War starts

1848 Mexican–American War ends. United States purchases New Mexico, Arizona, California, Utah, Nevada, and Texas

1850 Fugitive Slave Act

1860s Mass immigration from Poland

1861 American Civil War begins

1862 American Homestead Act provides settlers with free land in the Midwest

1863 Emancipation Proclamation frees slaves in Union-held territory

1865 American Civil War ends; all slaves freed

1868 The Fourteenth Amendment endows slaves with citizenship. Japanese laborers arrive in Hawaii

1870 The Fifteenth Amendment: African American males given the right to vote

1880s Mass immigration from Italy. Civil unrest and economic instability throughout Russia

1882 Chinese Exclusion Act

1887 The Dawes Act dissolves many Indian reservations in United States

1890s Start of mass immigration of Ukrainians to Canada

1891 Polygamists, the sick, and those convicted of "moral turpitude" made ineligible for immigration

1892 Ellis Island opens

1896 Supreme Court rules that "separate but equal" facilities for blacks and whites are constitutional

1898 The Spanish–American War begins. U.S. acquisition of Puerto Rico and Guam

1900 Jones Act grants U.S. citizenship to Puerto Ricans

1901 Anarchist Exclusion Act

1907 Expatriation Act. "Gentleman's Agreement" curtails Japanese immigration

1910 Mexican Revolution begins: thousands of Mexicans flee to the United States

1917 The United States enters World War I

1918 World War I ends

1921 Quota Act restricts the immigration of southern and eastern Europeans

1924 Johnson–Reed Act reduces fixed quota to 2 percent of nationality groups. Oriental Exclusion Act limits immigration from East Asia. U.S. Border Control created

1929 Congress makes annual immigration quotas permanent

1930s Mass deportation of Mexicans during the Great Depression

1939 World War II begins

1940 Alien Registration Act requires registration and fingerprinting of aliens

1942 Japanese Americans moved to "relocation camps." Bracero Program allows Mexican laborers to work in the United States

1943 Magnuson Act repeals Chinese Exclusion Act of 1882

1945 World War II ends.

1948 Displaced Persons Act permits European war refugees entry to the United States

1950 Internal Security Act bars entry of communists to the United States. Korean War begins

1952 McCarran–Walter Immigration Act removes race as a basis for exclusion

1953 Congress amends the 1948 refugee policy to admit more refugees. Korean War ends

1954 U.S. Supreme Court rules that "separate but equal" educational facilities are unconstitutional. Operation Wetback: INS deports more than 3 million people of Mexican heritage

1959 Cuban revolution

1962 Amendments to Canada's Immigration Act eliminate racial and religious discrimination

1964 Civil Rights Acts

1965 Immigration Act ends quota system. Bracero Program ends. Vietnam War begins

1966 Cuban Refugee Act admits more than 400,000 people to the United States

1971 Canadian government officially endorses policy of multiculturalism

1975 Vietnam War ends: mass immigration from Vietnam

1980 Refugee Act: 10 million permanent immigrants are legally admitted to the United States

1986 The Immigration Reform and Control Act (IRCA) raises annual immigration ceiling to 540,000

1990 Immigration Act allows 700,000 immigrants per year into the United States

1991 Persian Gulf War

1995 Canada officially endorses policy of First Nations self-government

1996 Immigration Act mandates the building of fences on U.S.–Mexico border

2002 Department of Homeland Security established

2003 U.S. forces attack Iraq

Numbers in **bold** refer to volume numbers; those in *italics* refer to picture captions.

Acadians *see* Cajuns and Acadians
Acoma Pueblo **1**:*31*
actors and actresses
   English American **4**:13
   Italian American **6**:16
Adams, John **5**:*40*; **6**:54
Addams, Jane **6**:62
adobe architecture **1**:*31, 32*; **8**:*6, 64*
affirmative action **9**:42, 68–69
Afghans **1**:*4*; **4**:7
African Americans **1**:*5–12*
   see also segregation and integration, slavery
   in broadcasting **2**:8
   cultural retention **3**:39
   discrimination against **5**:51
   families **4**:23
   festivals **1**:11; **2**:39; **4**:26
   housing **5**:18–19
   in industry and business **5**:48
   in literature **6**:64–65
   in local politics **7**:5
   in movies **4**:32
   and music **1**:*10, 12*; **4**:37
   newspapers and magazines **8**:23, *24*
   poverty **4**:61
   and Protestantism **9**:13–14
   return to Africa **9**:6; **10**:60
   shotgun houses **1**:*32*; **5**:18–19
   as slaves **1**:5, *7–8*, 11; **2**:36, 38; **3**:5–6; **5**:31, 49; **6**:52; **8**:28
   social mobility **9**:66–67
   and sports **1**:12; **9**:69; **10**:14–15
   stereotypes **1**:5; **9**:*8*
   and World War I **10**:55, *66*
   and World War II **10**:55–*56*, 68, 69
African Canadians **1**:*13–14*
Africans
   see also African Americans; African Canadians; East Africans; North Africans; South Africans; Southern Africans; West Africans
   crafts **3**:10
   folk medicine **5**:12, 13
   in Mexico **7**:18
   national loyalties **7**:38
   refugees **4**:6
   roots of American popular music **7**:34
Agassi, Andre **1**:*38*
agriculture **1**:*15–16*
   see also Bracero Program
   the Amish and **1**:*21*
   Belgians and **1**:61
   on the Great Plains **5**:49
   the Hutterites and **5**:26
   the Japanese and **6**:20
   Sikh farmers **9**:49
Alabama **10**:18
   Native Americans, Southeast **7**:68
Alamance, Battle of **9**:32
Alaska **10**:18
   Aleuts **1**:19–20
   border with Canada **3**:18
   and illegal immigration **3**:18
   Native Americans **4**:50; **7**:44–45, 66; **10**:34
   Russians **3**:7; **9**:24, 26
Alaska Native Claims Settlement Act (1971) **7**:66; **10**:34
Albanians **1**:*17–18*
Alberta, English **2**:*24*
Albright, Madaleine **3**:*44*
Aleuts **1**:19–20; **7**:44, *45*
   see also Inuit
Algerians **8**:32–33, *34*
Alien Act (1798) **8**:16
Alien and Sedition Acts (1798–1800) **1**:23, 24; **5**:40

Alien Enemies Act (1798) **8**:16
Aliens for Better Immigration Law **5**:16
Allende, Isabel **2**:51
Al Qaeda terrorist network **1**:4
America First Committee (AFC) **10**:67
American Indian Movement (AIM) **9**:54
American Indian Religious Freedom Act (1978) **8**:10
American Revolution (War of Independence) **1**:8; **3**:6, 17; **4**:11
   the French and **4**:44
   the Irish and **5**:65
   Loyalists **9**:15
   the Scotch-Irish and **9**:30, 33
American Samoans **8**:40
Amish **1**:*21–22*; **3**:52; **6**:42; **10**:25
   quilting **1**:*40*; **3**:10
Amity, Commerce and Navigation, Treaty of (1888) **7**:18
Anabaptists **1**:21; **7**:13; **9**:12
   see also Amish; Hutterites; Mennonites
Angel Island, California **5**:32, *34*
Anishinaabe *see* Chippewa
anti-immigrant discrimination *see* discrimination
anti-immigrant prejudice *see* prejudice
Apache **1**:*25–27*; **4**:23
Arab American Institute **8**:33
Arab Americans **1**:28–30
   see also Egyptians; Jordanians; Kuwaitis; Muslims; North Africans; Syrians
   newspapers **8**:24
Arapaho, Ghost Dance **4**:36
Arawaks **8**:66
architecture **1**:*31–32*
   see also housing
   adobe **1**:*31, 32*; **8**:*6, 64*
   Belgian **1**:62
   Danish **3**:45
   Norwegian **8**:*36*
   Spanish **10**:13
   Ukrainian **10**:*44*
Argentines **1**:*33–35*
Arizona **10**:18
   Native Americans, Southwest **8**:5
Arkansas **10**:18
Arlington, Virginia, Bolivians **1**:66
Armenians **1**:*36–38*; **4**:5
Armstrong, Louis **1**:*12*
Arnaz, Desi, Jr. **3**:41
art **1**:*39–40*
   see also architecture; crafts; literature
   Javacheff (Christo) **2**:9
Articles of Confederation **6**:54
Asian American Citizenship Act (1946) **1**:41
Asian Indians **1**:*41–44*
   see also Sikhs; Sri Lankans
   dress **3**:52, 53
   employment of **5**:34
   Hinduism **5**:20; **9**:13
Asians **7**:31
   see also Central Asians; East Asians
   families **4**:22–23
   and local politics **7**:5
   refugees **4**:6–7
   repatriated **9**:15–16
   trades and professions **10**:36
   U.S. citizenship **9**:67
assimilation **1**:*45–49*; **3**:34; **6**:10
   see also Native Americans, assimilation
   Danish **3**:47
   English **4**:13
   French **4**:46
   Germans **4**:53–54
   Japanese **6**:24
   Mexican **7**:24
   Russians and **9**:27
   Salvadorans and **9**:28–29
   Southern Africans **10**:7

Swedish **10**:23
Association of MultiEthnic Americans (AMEA) **7**:33
Athabascans (Dene Nation) **7**:44, *45*
Audubon, John James **4**:44
Australians **1**:*50*
Austrians **1**:*51–52*
Austro-Hungarian Empire **1**:51
   Croatians **3**:14
   Czechs **3**:42
   Hungary **5**:21–23
   Romanians **9**:*21*
   Slovaks **9**:61
   Ukraine **10**:42
Azerbaijanis **1**:*53–54*
Azikiwe, Nnamdi **10**:63
Aztecs **1**:*55–56*; **7**:17; **8**:6–7
   "writing" **6**:*54*

Back to Africa Movement **10**:60
Baer, Max **10**:*14*
Baha'is, in Iran **5**:60
Balanchine, George **4**:*51*
Balchen, Bernt **8**:38
Balkans **10**:8
Balkan Wars (1912–1913) **9**:*19*
Bangladeshis **1**:*57–58*
   see also Pakistanis
Bannock **7**:55, *56*
baptism, Mennonites and **7**:13
Baptists **9**:12
Barbadians **1**:*59–60*
barrio, el (Spanish Harlem) **8**:*68*, 69
Bartók, Béla **5**:23
Basques **7**:19; **10**:12
Batista, Fulgencio **3**:27
Batlle y Ordóñez, José **10**:47
Beirut **6**:*50*
Belarusians **2**:12
Belgians **1**:*61–62*
Belizeans **1**:*63*
Bell, Alexander Graham **9**:38, 39
Beothuk people **7**:49
Berlin, New Hampshire **10**:65
Berry, Halle **4**:32
Bienville, Jean-Baptiste **4**:41
bilingualism **6**:45
Bill of Rights, Canadian (1960) **1**:43
Binational Border Safety Initiative **3**:26
Black Codes **9**:6
Blackfeet **1**:*64–65*; **7**:*49, 58, 59*
Black Panthers **3**:34
Black Power movement **10**:37
"blacks," definition **9**:7
Bloods and Crips (gangs) **3**:13
boat people **5**:7; **10**:51, 53
Bolden, Buddy **1**:12
Bolivians **1**:*66–67*
Border Patrol, U.S. **3**:*19–24*
Borge, Victor **3**:*47*
Boskailo, Esad **1**:*68*
Bosnians **1**:*68–69*; **4**:6
Boston, Massachusetts
   Armenians **1**:37
   Brazilians **2**:5
   Irish Americans **5**:63
   Jews **6**:26
Bourbons **6**:10–12
Bracero Program **3**:23, 25; **7**:20, 23
Brazilians **2**:*4–6*
Britain *see* Great Britain
British Columbia
   African Canadians **1**:14
   English **2**:24
   Native Americans, Northwest Coast **7**:65
British Guiana **4**:68
British North America Act (1867) **2**:26, 29
broadcasting **2**:*7–8*; **6**:60
Bronck, Jonas **3**:45

Brown v. Board of Education (1954) **1**:10; **3**:66; **9**:9, 41, 67
Buddhism, Cambodians and **2**:17
buffalo **1**:64; **7**:58–60
Bulgarians **2**:*9–10*
Bureau of Indian Affairs (BIA) **3**:38; **8**:6, 10–11; **9**:17
Burmese **2**:11
Bury My Heart at Wounded Knee **6**:63–64
Bush, George W. **3**:19; **5**:15, 30, 39; **7**:*42*
Byelorussians **2**:12

Cabot, John **2**:25
Cabrillo, João Rodrigues **8**:61
Cajuns and Acadians **2**:*13–16*; **4**:44; **6**:55; **7**:35
California **10**:18
   African Americans **1**:6
   agriculture **1**:16; **4**:27; **5**:33; **9**:49
   Armenians **1**:37
   Asians and local politics **7**:5
   Bolivians **1**:67
   Cambodians **2**:18
   Chileans **2**:*51*
   Chinese **2**:52, *53, 54*, 59, 60; **9**:67
   Colombians **2**:*68*
   Costa Ricans **3**:9
   Cubans **3**:28
   Dutch **3**:64
   Finns **4**:34
   French **2**:31; **4**:45
   Gold Rush **1**:50; **4**:45
   Guatemalans **4**:*67*
   Hondurans **5**:17
   illegal immigrants **5**:30
   and intermarriage **5**:51
   Iranians **5**:60
   Japanese **6**:21
   Jews **6**:26
   Koreans **6**:34
   linguistic diversity **6**:45, 60
   Native Americans **7**:46–48; **8**:13
   Nicaraguans **8**:27
   Pacific Islanders **8**:41
   Panamanians **8**:48
   Paraguayans **8**:51
   Peruvians **8**:55
   Spanish **10**:13
   Swiss **10**:26
   Vietnamese in **10**:51
Calusa **7**:67
Cambodians **2**:*17–18*; **5**:20
Canada
   border with Alaska **3**:18
   crossborder migration **3**:17–20; **5**:30
   Cuban trade with **3**:29
   Dominion of **2**:26
   emigration from **2**:22
   and the French **4**:*43*
   Great Seal of **2**:29
   immigration/emigration **2**:*19–22*; **5**:33
   and interfaith marriage **5**:53
   literacy in **6**:60
   local politics **6**:68–69
   multiculturalism **2**:21; **7**:30–31
   national politics **7**:39–*40*
   Nunavut **5**:58; **7**:31, 51; **8**:15
   oath of citizenship to **2**:19
   prime ministers **7**:40
   and religion **9**:11–12
   slavery **9**:58
   Ukrainians **10**:42
   and urban reform **10**:46
   and World Wars I and II **10**:56, 64, 68
Canadian Indian Act (1876) **7**:51
Canadians
   African **1**:*13–14*
   Armenian **1**:38
   Asian Indians **1**:41, 42, 43
   Australian **1**:50
   Austrians **1**:52
   Brazilians **2**:5

Cajuns 2:14
Cambodians 2:18
Chinese 2:53
Chinese (overseas) 2:59
Dutch 3:57
Egyptians 3:69
English 2:23–29
Filipinos 4:27, 28
Finns 4:33, 34
French 2:19, 21, 30–35; 4:42
Germans 4:54
Haida 5:6
Hawaiians 5:11
Hungarians 5:22
Icelanders 5:28
Indo-Fijians 8:40–42
Inuit 5:55
Iroquois Confederacy 6:5
Israelis 6:9
Italians 6:10
Japanese 5:33; 6:21
Jews 6:30
Koreans 6:35
Libyans 8:34
Lithuanians 6:67
Maltese 7:8
Mennonites 7:14
Métis 7:15–16
Mexicans 7:20, 22, 23
Mormons 7:29
Native Americans 7:49–51
Norwegians 8:36, 37
Pakistanis 8:43, 44
Poles 8:57
Portuguese 8:62
Romanians 9:22
Russians 9:26–27
Sikhs 9:49, 50
Slovaks 9:59
South Africans 10:4
Southern Africans 10:6, 7
South Slavs 10:9
Spanish 10:10, 11, 13
Sri Lankans 10:16
Swedes 10:21
Swiss 10:26
Syrians 10:28
Thais 10:31
Tlingits 10:34
Trinidadians and Tobagonians 10:38
Turkish 10:40, 41
Ukrainian 10:42–44
Vietnamese 10:52, 54
Welsh 10:59
West Africans 10:61
Capone, Alphonse ("Al") 3:12; 6:15
Carey, Mariah 7:32
Caribana festival 10:38
Caribbean peoples 2:36–37; 4:7–8
    see also Barbadians; Cubans;
        Dominicans; Jamaicans; Puerto
        Ricans; Trinidadians and
        Tobagonians
Carignan, Jean 2:32
Carmichael, Stokely 10:37
Carnegie, Andrew 9:39
carnivals, Caribbean 2:36, 37
Carrere, Tia 4:29
Carter, Jimmy 8:47
Cartier, Jacques 2:30; 4:41
Carver, George Washington 1:15
casinos 8:6; 9:18
Casquelourd, Malonga 2:40
castes 1:43
Catawba 7:67, 68
Catholicism see Roman Catholicism
Catlin, George 1:64
Caucasians, North 2:45
Central Africans 2:38–41
Central Asians 2:42–44
    see also Afghans; Armenians;
        Russians; Turks
Cernan, Eugene A. 9:62

Chamorros 8:40
Champlain, Samuel de 2:13, 32; 4:41, 49
Chanute, Octave 4:45
Chaplin, Charlie 4:31
Charter of Rights and Freedoms (1982:
    Canada) 7:15
Chávez, César E. 1:16; 6:40; 7:24
Chávez, Hugo 10:49
Chechens 2:45–46
Cherokee 2:47–49; 7:68; 9:6, 11
    language 2:47–49; 6:44
    Trail of Tears 2:49; 7:67
Chiang Kai-shek 2:60
Chicago, Illinois 2:64; 4:61; 10:17, 18
    Arab Americans 1:29
    black population 9:42
    Bosnians 1:68
    Brazilians 2:5
    industry 5:48, 49
    Jews 6:26
    Serbians 9:46
    Swedes 10:23, 24
Chicano Movement 7:24
Chicanos 1:24; 7:24
Chickasaw 7:68, 69
children 1:46–47
    see also education
Chileans 2:50–51
Chinatowns 2:52; 3:32, 41; 10:36
Chinese 2:52–57; 5:32, 49
    businesses 10:36
    discrimination against 9:67
    and the family 4:22
    illegal immigration via Mexico 3:22
    immigrants detained 5:32, 34
    immigration suspended 1:24; 2:20,
        54; 5:32, 41, 42, 48
    medicine 5:12, 13
    in Mexico 7:19
    national loyalties 7:38
    New Year 2:56–57; 3:41; 4:25
    Taiwanese 2:59, 60–61
    "tongs" 3:12, 35
Chinese Exclusion Act (1882) 1:24; 5:32,
    41, 42; 9:67
Chinese Immigration Service 3:22
Chinese Six Companies 2:55
Chinh, Kieu 2:58
Chippewa (Ojibwa; Anishinabe)
    2:62–63; 7:61; 9:52
Chisholm, Shirley 1:59
Choctaw 7:68, 69
Chopra, Deepak 1:42, 43
Chrétien, Jean 7:40
Christianity 9:11–13
Chumash 5:18
Ch'usok 6:36
Cinco de Mayo festival 4:26, 38; 7:37
cities, U.S. 2:64–65
citizenship 5:40
    ceremonies 4:53; 5:32, 38
    for Native Americans 9:67
civil rights
    black 1:9–10
    Mexican American 7:24
    power movements 3:35
Civil Rights Act (1964) 3:53; 9:68
Civil War, U.S. 2:38; 5:48; 9:58; 10:55, 58
    African Americans 1:8; 9:58
Clarkson, Adrienne 2:56
Clemente, Roberto 8:68
Cleveland, Ohio, Slovenes 9:64
clothes see dress and costume
Code Talkers, Navajo 6:57
Cold War
    and Bulgarians 2:9
    and ethnicity 2:66
Cold/Hot Weather campaigns 3:26
Cole, Nat King 3:41
Cole, Thomas 1:39, 40
Colombians 2:67–69
colonial America 3:4–6
Colorado 10:18

color, definitions of 9:7
Color Purple, The (Walker) 6:64–65
Columbus, Christopher 9:12
Comanche, and trickster figures 9:11
communists
    communist witch-hunts 4:32; 8:18
    Red Scare and 6:14–15; 8:18
communities, immigrant 1:46
Congress, U.S. 7:42
    Cuban representatives 3:29
Connecticut 10:18
    Slovaks 9:60
Constitution, U.S. 7:41
Cooper, James Feinmore 6:63
Coptic immigrants 3:68
Cortés, Hernán 1:56; 7:18
Cosby, Bill 2:8
Cossacks 3:7
Costa Ricans 3:8–9
costume see dress and costume
cotton 5:48, 49; 9:56
coureurs des bois 2:32; 4:43
cowboys 1:16
crafts 1:20; 3:10–11; 10:33
    see also art; stonecarving
Creeks see Seminole and Creeks
Creole 6:43
crime
    ethnic 3:12–13
    on reservations 9:18
    and the U.S.-Canadian law
        enforcement coalition 3:17
Croatian Workers' Benefit Society
    3:14–16
Croatians 3:14–16; 10:8–9
    Bosnian Croats 1:68
Crockett, David "Davy" 9:34
cross-border migration
    Canadian 3:17–20; 5:30
    Mexican 3:21–26; 5:30
Crow 5:18
Cubans 3:27–29; 4:8, 22
Culloden, Battle of 9:37
cultural borderlands 3:30–32
cultural mingling 3:31–32, 33–36
    English culture 4:13–14
    French culture 4:46–47
cultural retention 1:45–46; 3:34, 37–41
    see also language retention; national
        loyalties
    Arabic 1:30
    Cajun 2:16
    Caribbean 2:37
    East African 3:62
    German 4:57
    Italian Mafia 3:13
    Korean 6:36
    Latvians 6:49
    Native American 3:38
    Pacific Islanders 8:42
    Polish 8:59
cultural tension 3:34–35
Czechs 3:42–44
    see also Slovaks

Dalai Lama 4:7; 10:32
dancing and dances
    Asian Indian 1:41
    Costa Rican 3:9
    Croatian 3:16
    flamenco 10:13
    French influences 4:47
    Greek 4:64
    Hungarian 5:25
    Irish 5:65
    Jamaican 6:19
    Métis 7:15
    Mexican 7:25
    Native American 7:49, 57
    Pacific Islanders 8:42
    Polynesian 5:10
    salsa 3:39
    Scottish 9:35

step dancing 7:16
    tango 1:35
    Ukrainian 10:42, 44
Danes 3:45–48
Davies, Robertson 6:65
Dawes, Henry L., and the Dawes Act
    1:46; 8:10
Day of the Dead 4:24; 7:37–38
Day of the Three Kings 1:33
Day of Tradition 1:33
Delaware 10:18
    Native Americans, Northeast 7:62
Dene Nation see Athabascans
Department of Indian Affairs 9:17
deportation 5:42
    see also repatriation
Depression see Great Depression
Detroit, Michigan
    Arab Americans 1:29
    Bangladeshis 1:57, 58
    Poles 8:59
Dia de los Muertos, El, see Day of the
    Dead
diaspora
    Armenian 1:36
    Jewish 6:25–27
Diaz, Manny 2:5
Diné College 8:21
"Dirty War" 1:33
discrimination, anti-immigrant 5:32; 9:40
    see also prejudice; segregation and
        integration
    against African Americans 5:51
    against the Japanese 5:31, 33; 6:22,
        23; 8:18
    against Palestinians 8:46
    and ethnic neighborhoods 9:7–8
Displaced Persons Act (1948) 2:66; 5:43;
    9:23
District of Columbia 10:18
    see also Washington, D.C.
Diwali 1:41
Dominicans 3:49–50
Dominion Land Act (1872) 2:19; 10:21
Dorsey, Thomas A. 1:10
Douglas, Kirk 8:52
Douglass, Frederick 6:64; 9:57
dress and costume 3:51–53; 7:37
    see also fashion
    Bavarian 4:58
    Latvian 6:48
    Mayan 7:10, 11
    Mennonite 7:13
    Moroccan 8:30
    Native American 7:48, 64
    Norwegian 8:39
    Polish 8:58, 60
    Romany 5:4
    Spanish 5:10
    Vietnamese 10:54
    Zapotec 7:19
drug smuggling, cross-border 3:20, 24;
    5:29
Du Bois, W.E.B. 3:66; 6:64
du Pont, E.I. 4:41
Dutch, the 3:5, 54–58
Duvalier, "Papa Doc" 5:7

East Africans 3:59–62; 5:36
    see also Ethiopians; Somalians
East Asians
    see also Burmese; Laotians;
        Vietnamese
    refugees 4:6–7
Ecuadoreans 3:63–64
Edison, Thomas 9:34, 39
education 3:65–67
    see also literacy
    Asian Indians and 1:44
    Central Africans and 2:40
    Chinese and 2:56
    cultural mingling in schools 3:32
    desegregation in 9:67, 68

Dominicans and 3:50
East Africans and 3:61
English and 4:15
Finnish and 4:35
Irish and 5:68
Jews and 6:30
Mennonites and 7:14
multiculturalism and 7:30
in the native language 6:45
Pacific Islanders 8:42
segregation in 3:66; 6:22; 9:41, 43
Slovaks and 9:61–62
and social mobility 9:65, 67–68
Southern Africans and 10:5
statistics 9:67
Egyptians 1:28–30; 3:68–69
1812, War of 1:13; 3:20
Einstein, Albert 4:53
El Salvador, people see Salvadorans
Ellis Island 1:24, 49; 3:42; 4:19; 5:43
deportations from 5:42
medical examinations 5:13, 42
Emancipation Proclamation (1863) 1:8, 11
emigrés and refugees 4:4–8; 5:34
anticommunist refugees 4:8; 5:39
Armenian 1:36; 4:5
Byelorussian 2:12
Cambodian 2:17
Cossack 3:7
Latvian 6:48–49
as returnees 9:19
Southern African refugees 10:7
Tibetan refugees 10:32
to Canada 2:21–22
Vietnamese refugees 10:51–53
and World War II see World War II
employment see industry and employment
English 4:9–15
in colonial America 3:4–5; 4:9–11
houses 3:10
racial attitudes 9:5–6, 8–9
sports 4:15; 10:14
English Only laws and movements 6:54, 59
Erasmus, Georges 7:51
Eritreans 3:59
Eskimos 5:54; 7:44, 45
Estonians 4:16
see also Latvians; Lithuanians
Ethiopians 3:59; 4:4, 17
slaves from 3:61
ethnicity, multiple, see multiple ethnic origins
eugenics 9:8
Europeans 4:49
eastern European Jews 6:28–29
family patterns 4:20–21
and the frontier 4:50
and medicine 5:13–14
and music 7:35
national loyalties 7:37
trades and professions 10:35–36
types of immigrant 4:18–20
Evangeline (Longfellow) 2:15
Executive Order 9981 10:56
explorers 4:41, 44, 50; 6:11; 8:61; 10:10–12

Fair Housing Act (1968) 4:61
Fairclough, Ellen 2:21
family patterns 1:49; 4:18–23
Asian-Indian 1:43
Cambodian 2:18
East African 3:62
and ghetto life 4:61
Jewish 6:30–31
Mexican 7:24
North African 8:35
Puerto Rican 8:69
Romany 5:4
Salvadoran 9:29

Taiwanese 2:61
farming see agriculture
fashion
African-American 1:11
French 4:47
federalism 7:41
festivals 4:24–26
Fifteenth Amendment 7:41; 9:66
Fifty-Sixers 5:23
Fijians 8:40
Filipinos 1:16; 4:23, 27–30
film 4:31–32
emigrés in Hollywood 4:5
Mexicans and 7:25
names of movie stars 8:52
Finns 4:22, 33–35
First Amendment 9:12
First Nations people 7:49–51
Fitzgerald, Ella 3:41
Five Civilized Tribes 2:47
Florida 10:18
Argentines in 1:34
Bolivians 1:67
Chileans 2:51
Colombians 2:68
Costa Ricans 3:9
Cubans 3:28
Dominicans 3:50
Dutch 3:64
Finns 4:34
French 2:31
Guatemalans 4:67
Hondurans 5:17
Jews 6:26
Native Americans, Southeast 7:68
Nicaraguans 8:27
Pacific Islanders 8:41
Panamanians 8:48
Paraguayans 8:51
Peruvians 8:55
Spanish 10:12
Venezuelans 10:50
folklore 4:36–38
food and drink 4:39–40
Argentinian 1:34, 35
Caribbean 1:60; 2:37
Chinese 2:53, 56; 3:30
English Canadian 2:23, 24
"fast food" 4:39, 40
French 4:42, 46, 47
French Canadian 2:31, 34, 35
"fusion food" 4:40
German 4:54, 58
kosher 3:30; 6:28, 29
Native American 2:48, 63
"soul food" 4:40; 10:62
Foran Act (1885) 6:12–13
Forman, Milos 3:44
Fort Nassau, New York 3:54
Fort Wayne, Indiana 2:11
Forty-Eighters 4:55
Forty-Niners 5:23
Fourteenth Amendment 7:41; 9:67
Franklin, Benjamin 6:6; 9:66
free speech, right of 7:43
Freedom Riders 9:41
French 1:31; 4:41–47
French and Indian War 2:32; 3:17; 4:44
Battle of the Plains of Abraham (Battle of Quebec) 2:32–33; 3:17
French Guyanese 4:48
French Revolution 4:44
Front de Libération du Quebéc (FLQ) 6:68, 69; 9:4
frontier 4:49–52; 5:31–32, 49
Scotch-Irish and 9:32
Fugitive Slave Bill (1850) 9:58
fur traders 4:43, 49; 7:15; 8:8

Gajdusek, Carleton Daniel 9:61
Galarza, Ernesto 7:23
Gallaudet, Thomas 4:43
gangs 3:13, 35

Garibaldi, Giuseppe 6:10
Garifuna 5:16, 17
Garvey, Marcus 9:6; 10:60
General Allotment Act (1887; Dawes Act) 1:46; 8:10
Gentlemen's Agreement (1907) 6:22, 35
Georgians 4:51–52
Georgia 10:18
Panamanians 8:48
Germans 4:53–59; 5:41, 47–48
Jews 6:27–28
language 6:54, 59, 60
"superior" race 9:8–9
and World War I 10:65
Germantown, Pennsylvania 4:55, 56; 7:13
Germany, Nazi 4:5, 56; 5:4; 6:28, 29
Geronimo 1:27
Ghanaians 10:63
Ghent, Treaty of (1814) 3:20
ghettos 4:60–61; 9:42
Ghost Dance 4:36
Giuliani, Rudolph 6:13
Godfather, The (novel and movies) 3:12; 4:32
Gold Rush, California 2:50; 4:45
Golem story 4:37, 38
Gomes, Estévão 8:61
Gompers, Samuel 6:40
González, Elian 3:27
González, Rodolfo "Corky" 7:24
Gore, Al 6:42; 7:42, 43
Go Tell It on the Mountain (Baldwin) 6:64
Graffenried, Christoph von 10:25
Graham, Billy 9:14
Great Awakenings 9:12
Great Britain
see also English; Scottish; Welsh
immigration from 5:41, 47
Great Depression 2:27; 7:23; 9:16
Great Plains
farming of 5:49
Native Americans 5:18; 7:58–60; 8:13
Greeks 4:62–64; 9:19
see also Macedonians
Greeley, Horace 9:34
Greenlanders 4:65
Inuit 4:65; 5:56
Gretzky, Wayne 8:60
Groulx, Lionel 9:4
Grundtvig, Frederik Lange 3:47
Guadalupe Hidalgo, Treaty of (1848) 7:21
Guam 8:40
Guarani 8:50, 51
Guatemalans 4:66–67
Mayans 4:66; 7:10, 11
Guess Who's Coming to Dinner (movie) 5:52
guild system 4:57
Gulf War 5:61
Gullah people 3:10
Guyanese 4:68–69
Guy, John 2:25
Gypsies (Romany) 5:4–5

Haida nation 5:6
Haitians 1:32; 5:7–9; 6:43; 9:20
Halloween 4:24–25, 37
Hamilton, Alexander 9:38–39
Handsome Lake 7:63
Hanson, John 10:21
Harambe 1:11; 2:39
Harlem, New York City 1:59; 4:60; 9:42, 66
Spanish Harlem (el barrio) 8:68
Harvard University 3:65; 4:14, 15
Haudenosaunee 6:4, 7
Hawaii 10:18
see also Honolulu
Filipino workers 4:28
Japanese 6:21
Pacific Islanders 8:41

Hawaiians 5:10–11
language 5:11; 6:45, 58
literacy 6:61
health and healing 4:22; 5:12–14
Haitian 5:9
medical examinations 5:13, 42
"hello girls" 10:64
Helsinki Accord (1974–1975) 9:23
Hendrix, Jimi 3:35, 41
Herrera, Ramon 9:69
Highland Clearances 9:37
Highland Games 3:53; 9:39
Hinduism 1:44; 5:20; 9:13
hip-hop culture 3:36
Hispanic Americans (Latinos) 5:15
see also Belizeans; French Guyanese;
Mexicans; Surinamese
architecture 1:32
Argentines 1:33–35
art 1:39
Bolivians 1:66–67
Brazilians 2:4–6
and broadcasting 2:8
Chileans 2:50–51
Colombians 2:67–69
Costa Ricans 3:8–9
Cubans 3:27–29; 4:8, 22
Dominicans 3:49–50
economic and political migration 3:25
Ecuadoreans 3:63–64
and the family 4:21–22
folklore 4:38
Guatemalans 4:66–67; 7:10, 11
Guyanese 4:68–69
Hondurans 5:16–17
and illegal immigration to Mexico 3:24–25
language retention 6:42
in local government 7:5
music 7:36
national loyalties 7:37–38
newspapers 8:24
Nicaraguans 8:26–29; 9:20
Paraguayans 8:50–51
Puerto Ricans 6:61; 7:35; 8:66–69; 9:66
refugees 4:7–8
Salvadorans 9:20, 28–29
Venezuelans 10:49–50
Hmong 3:10; 5:35–36; 6:46, 47
Hoffa, James R. 6:39
hogans 1:31
Holland, Michigan 3:57, 58
Hollywood
communist witch-hunts 4:32
emigrés in 4:5
Holy Roman Empire 4:55
Homeland Security, Department of 5:30, 39
Homestead Act (1862) 1:16; 3:42, 45; 5:49; 8:36; 10:21
Hondurans 5:16–17
Hong Kong 2:57, 59
Honolulu, Hawaii
Chinese 2:53
Pacific Islanders 8:41
Hooks, Benjamin 2:8
Hoover, Herbert 10:25
Hopi Pueblo 8:65
House Made of Dawn (Momaday) 7:58
House Un-American Activities Committee 4:32
housing 1:31; 5:18–20
see also architecture
in the colonies 3:6
in ghettos 4:60, 61
Inuit 5:54
log cabins 5:19
Native-American 1:26; 5:18; 6:6; 7:61, 63; 8:6; 9:44
public housing projects 4:61; 5:19–20
segregation in 9:42, 43
shotgun houses 1:32; 5:18–19
tenements 4:60; 5:19

Housing Act (1968) **9:**42
Housing and Urban Development, Department of **10:**45
Houston, Sam **9:***34*
Houston, Texas, Brazilians **2:**5
How the Other Half Lives (Riis) **2:**65
hoyaneh **6:**5–6
Huckleberry Finn (Twain) **6:**64
Hudson, Henry **3:**54
Hudson River School **1:**40
Hughes, Langston **6:**64
Huguenots **4:**43, 45, 47
Hull House **6:**62
Hungarian Revolution (1956) **5:***21,* 22
Hungarians **5:***21–25*
Hurons **4:**49; **7:**49, 61, *62,* 63
Hussein, Saddam **5:**61, 62; **6:**37
Hutterites **3:**52; **5:***26–27;* **6:**42

Icelanders **5:**28
Idaho **10:**18
    Native Americans, Columbia Plateau **7:**53
illegal immigration **5:***29–30,* 34, *37, 44*
    see also repatriation
    to Alaska **3:**18
    Bangladeshis **1:**57, 58
    Brazilian **2:**4, 6
    Colombians **2:**67
    Ecuadorians **3:**64
    from Canada **3:***19,* 20
    from Mexico **3:**18, 21, 23–25; **5:***30,* 34; **7:***21,* 23
    "OTMs" (Other Than Mexicans) **3:**21
Illinois **4:**43; **10:**18
    Cubans **3:**28
    Czechs **3:**43
    Dutch **3:**64
    Guatemalans **4:**67
    Japanese **6:**21
    Jews **6:**26
    Koreans **6:**34
    Native Americans, Northeast **7:**62
    Paraguayans **8:**51
    Slovaks **9:**60
illnesses, and ethnicity **7:**33
immigrant experience **5:***31–36*
Immigration Act
    of 1907 (U.S.) **3:***22–23*
    of 1910 (Canada) **1:**14
    of 1917 (U.S.) **3:**23; **6:**61
    of 1924 (U.S.; National Origins Act; Johnson–Reed Act) **2:**40; **5:**43; **6:**12, 13; **8:**18
    of 1962 (Canada) **1:**43
    of 1965 (U.S.) **2:**40, 60; **4:**62; **6:**33, 35; **8:**43
    of 1990 (U.S.) **2:**40; **8:**43
Immigration and Nationality Act (1952) *see* McCarran-Walter Act
Immigration and Naturalization Service (INS) **5:**29, *37–39*
immigration legislation, U.S. **5:***40–44*
Immigration Reform and Control Act (1986) **5:***29–30,* 44
Imperial Valley, California **1:**16; **4:**27
Independence, War of, *see* American Revolution
Indiana **10:**18
    Amish population **1:**22
Indian Citizenship Act (1924) **9:**67
Indian Defense Association **9:**9
Indian Defense League of America **9:**50
Indian Removal Act (1830) **2:**49; **4:**50; **9:***32*
Indian Reorganization Act (1934) **7:**48; **9:**17
Indian Territory **2:**49; **7:**67, 69
Indians, Asian, *see* Asian Indians
Indo-Fijians **8:***40–42*
Indochina, refugees from **4:**6
Indonesians **5:***45–46*
Industrial Workers of the World **6:***39*

industry and employment **5:***32–33, 47–49*
    see also labor unions; trades and professions
    Italian **6:**13
    Jews **6:**30
    Korean **6:***35–36*
    Native Americans and **6:**7; **8:**8
    Nigerians **8:**28
    Pacific Islanders **8:**42
    Puerto Ricans **8:**69
    railroad workers **2:**54; **4:**50; **9:***49*
    Swedes **10:***21,* 23
Inouye, Daniel Ken **6:**23
INS *see* Immigration and Naturalization Service
Intergovernmental Agencies for Refugees (IAR) **4:**4
intermarriage **4:***20,* 23; **5:***50–53*
    see also mestizos; Metis; multiple ethnic origins
Internet, languages and the **6:**41
Intifadah **6:**9
Inuit **4:**65; **5:***54–58;* **7:**51
    see also Aleuts
Inupiats **7:**44
Inuvialuit **5:**57
Iowa **10:**18
    Czechs **3:**43
Iran–Contra affair **8:**27
Iranians **4:**7; **5:***59–60*
    see also Kurds
Iraqis **1:**30; **4:**7; **5:***61–62*
    see also Kurds
Irish **5:**32, 41, 47, *63–69*
    employment **10:**35
    in the Mexican-American War **7:**19
    and politics **5:***68–69;* **7:***4–5*
    prejudice against **1:**23; **5:**41, 65; **8:**17
    repatriated **9:**15
    and World War I **10:**65
Iroquois Confederacy **4:**49; **6:***4–7;* **7:**63; **9:**11
Ishi **7:**48
Israel **8:**45
    and Syria **10:**28
Israelis **6:***8–9*
    see also Palestinians
Italians **3:**37; **4:***19;* **6:***10–16;* **10:**35
    and Catholicism **9:***12*
    and the Mafia **3:***12–13;* **4:**32
    temporary workers **9:**16
Italo-Turkish War **8:**33

Jackson, Andrew **9:***32*
Jackson, Jesse **7:**5
Jamaicans **6:***17–19*
James I, *king of England* **9:**30
Jamestown, Virginia **3:**4, *6;* **4:***9,* 55; **9:**12
    African Americans in **1:***5–7*
    Poles in **8:**56
    slaves **9:**6, 55
Japan, and Mexico **7:**18
Japanese **5:**42; **6:***20–24*
    discrimination against **1:***23;* **5:***31, 33;* **6:**22, 23; **8:***18*
    dress **3:***51*
    and the family **4:***22–23*
    farmers **1:**16
    and music **7:**36
    and World War I **10:**55, 56
    and World War II **1:**23; **2:**20; **5:***31, 33;* **6:**22, 23; **9:***20;* **10:**55, 56, *67–68*
Javacheff, Christo **2:**9
Javanese **8:**45
Jesuits **4:***44*
Jews **1:**45; **3:**30; **6:***25–31*
    and the Nazis **4:**5, 56; **6:**29; **10:**36
    folklore **4:**37, 38
    food and drink **3:**30; **6:**28, 29, *31*
    from Israel **6:**8
    German **4:**56; **10:***35–36*
    Jewish American writers **6:**65

marriage and weddings **4:***20*
    in Mexico **7:**18
    moviemakers **4:**32
    New Year festival **4:**25; **6:***30*
    Orthodox **9:***11,* 13
    Polish **8:**56
    Reform **9:**13
    repatriated **9:**16
    as returnees **9:**19
    Russian/Soviet **5:**36; **7:**18; **9:**26, 27
    Sephardic **6:**27
Jim Crow laws **9:**40
Johnson, Lyndon B. **2:**40
Johnson–Reed Act *see* Immigration Act, of 1924
Johnston, George **10:**34
Jolliet, Louis **4:**41
Jolson, Al **4:**32; **9:**8
Jones, Marion **1:**63
Jordanians **6:**32
    see also Palestinians
Jordan, Michael **9:**68
Judaism **6:**25, 30
Jumper, Betty Mae **9:**45
Juneteenth **1:**11; **2:**39; **4:**26

Kachina festivals **8:**65
Kanjobal communities **4:**67
Kansas **10:**18
Kashmir **8:**44
Kawaiisu **7:**55, *56*
Kee, Sing **10:**65
Kendall Township **8:**36
Kennedy, John F. **3:**68; **5:***66–67*
Kentucky **10:**18
Kenya **3:**59, 60, 62
Kerouac, Jack **2:**35
Khannouchi, Khalid **8:**32
Khmer Rouge **2:**17, 18
Khomeini, Ruhollah **5:**60
Kikuyu people **3:**61
King, Martin Luther, Jr. **1:**9, 10; **9:**13, *41–43*
King William's War **3:**17
Kingston, Maxine Hong **2:**55
Kissinger, Henry **4:**59
kivas **1:**31
Know-Nothings **8:**17
Koreans **5:**14; **6:***33–36;* **10:**36
Korean War **6:**33, 35; **10:**56
Kosovo **1:**18; **9:**48
Ku Klux Klan **1:***8–9;* **5:**51; **8:**18
Kurds **6:**37
Kuwaitis **6:**38
Kwanzaa **1:**11; **2:**39

labor unions **6:***39–40*
Lafitte, Jean **2:**15
Land Claims Settlement Act (1971) **7:**45
land rights, native peoples and **4:**50; **5:**11; **6:**7; **7:**46; **8:***9–11*
language
    see also language retention; linguistic groups
    American slang **5:**33
    Central African influence **2:**41
    Cherokee **2:***47–49;* **6:**44
    and cultural mingling **3:**33
    Diné (Navajo) **8:**21
    Dutch **3:***57–58*
    English **6:**61
    English Only laws and movements **6:**54, 59
    Filipino **5:**30
    French **4:**46; **6:**54, 60
    German **6:**54, 59, 60
    Hawaiian **5:**11; **6:**45, 58
    Hungarian **5:**22
    Icelandic **5:**28
    Inuit **5:**55
    Jewish **6:**26
    learning English **5:**33, *34–35;* **6:***10,* 27
    Maya **4:**67

Native Americans and **6:***42–45,* 55–58, 61; **7:**47; **8:**14, 21, 65
Norwegian **8:**39
Pacific Islanders **8:**41
Serbo-Croatian **9:**48
Spanish **6:**55, 59, 60
language retention **6:***41–45*
    by Aleuts **1:**20
    by Chechens **2:**45
    Cajun **2:**16
    Canadian bilingualism **2:***19,* 21, 23–25
    Canadian English **2:***28–29*
    languages spoken at home **6:**56
    Swahili **3:**59
Lansbury, Angela **4:***15*
Laotians **6:***46–47*
Laporte, Pierre **6:**68, 69; **9:**4
La Salle, Robert Cavelier de **4:**41
Last of the Mohicans, The (Cooper) **6:***63*
Latin Americans *see* Hispanic Americans
Latinidad **3:**40
Latinismo **3:**40
Latvians **6:***48–49*
    see also Estonians; Lithuanians
Laurel, Stan **4:**14
Leacock, Stephen **6:**65
Lebanese **1:**28; **6:***50–51*
    see also Palestinians
Lee, Sammy **6:**36
Lee, Spike **4:**32
Leguizamo, John **2:**69
Lévesque, René **9:**4
Lewis and Clark expedition **4:**50
Lewis, John Llewellyn **10:**58
Lexington, Battle of **9:**30
Liberians **6:***52–53;* **10:**60
Libyans **8:***33–34,* 35
Lincoln, Abraham **8:***53;* **9:***57–58;* **10:**58
Lindbergh, Charles **10:**23
linguistic groups **6:***54–58*
literacy **6:***59–61*
    see also education
Literacy Test (1917) **5:**42
literature **6:***62–65*
    Italian American writers **6:**16
    Jews and **6:**31
    Mexican **7:**25
Lithuanians **6:***66–67*
    see also Estonians; Latvians
Little Bighorn, Battle of the **9:***17,* 54
Little Italies **6:**10, *12;* **10:**35
Little Norway homestead **8:**36
Little Odessa **9:**26
lobbying, political **7:**38
Lockerbie bombing **8:**33
Lodge, Henry Cabot **1:**24
Longfellow, H.W. **2:**15; **6:**62
"Long-House Religion" **7:**63
long houses **7:**61, *63;* **10:**33
Long March **8:**21
Lopez, Jennifer **8:**69
Los Angeles, California **2:**65; **4:**61; **10:**18
    Argentines **1:***34*
    Armenians **1:**36
    Brazilians **2:**5
    Cambodians **2:***18*
    Chinatown **3:**32
    Chinese **2:**53
    Japanese **6:***20*
    Jews **6:**26
    Koreans **6:**26
    Koreatown **6:**35, 36
    Pacific Islanders **8:***41*
Lott, Trent **9:**42
Louisiana **4:**43; **10:**18
    see also New Orleans
    Cajuns and Acadians **2:***13–15,* 16
    French **2:**31
Louisiana Purchase **3:**17; **4:**44; **5:**49; **6:**60
Louis, Joe **10:**14
luaus **5:**11
lunch counters, segregated **9:**41
Lutherans **10:**24

Luther, Martin **4:**55, 58
Lyfoung, Nkauj'lis **6:**46

MacDonalds **5:**39
Macedonians **7:**6
Mack, Charles **9:***8*
Madeira **8:**63
Mafia **3:***12–13;* **4:***32;* **6:**14, 15
magazines *see* newspapers and
    magazines
Magyars **5:**21
Maine **10:**18
    Canadian border **3:***17–18*
    Native Americans, Northeast **7:**62
Malaeska (dime novel) **6:**62
Malaysians **7:**7
    see also Singaporeans
Malecite people **7:**49
Maltese **7:***8*
Manhattan Island, purchase **3:***54–56*
Manifest Destiny **3:**38; **4:**49; **9:**7
Mankiller, Wilma P. **2:**49
Mao Tse-tung **2:**60
maquiladoras **3:**31
Marcantonio, Vito **6:**16
Marcos, Sub-Commandante **7:**11; **8:**7
Mardi Gras **4:**24, *47*
Mariel Boat Lift **3:**27
Marin, Rosario **9:**69
Marquette, Jacques **4:**41, *44*
marriage(s)
    see also intermarriage; war brides;
        weddings
    arranged **1:**44, 58; **5:**35; **8:***43*
    Japanese picture brides **6:**22
    Mennonites and **7:**13
Marsalis, Wynton **7:**34
Marshall Plan **4:**59
"Martin the Armenian" **1:**37
Maryland **10:**18
    anti-Irish prejudice **1:**23
    Jews **6:**26
    Paraguayans **8:***51*
Masai people **3:**62
Masaryk, Tomás **3:**44; **9:**59
Massachusetts **10:**18
    see also Boston; Provincetown
    Cambodians **2:***18*
    Chinese **2:***53*
    Dominicans **3:***50*
    Finns **4:***34*
    French **2:**31
    Jews **6:**26
    Massachusetts Bay Colony **9:**12, 15
    Plymouth colony **3:**4
Mauritians **7:**9
Mayans **4:**66; **7:***10–11, 17;* **8:***6–7*
    and Zapatistas **8:**7, 15
Mayflower Compact **3:**4
Mayflower (ship) **3:***4*
McCarran–Walter Act (Immigration
    and Naturalization/Nationality Act;
    1952) **2:**54, 66; **3:**23; **4:**28; **5:***43–44;*
    6:23; **10:**5
McCarthy, Joseph **8:**18
media, mass
    see also broadcasting; newspapers
    and cultural mingling **3:**34
medical examinations, for immigrants
    5:*13, 42*
medicine
    see also health and healing
    alternative **1:***43*
medicine men (shamans) **1:***64;* **5:**56;
    10:33
Meech Lake Accord (1987) **9:**4
Mehta, Zubin **5:**53
Melanesia **8:**40
Mellon, Andrew **9:**34
"melting pot" **1:**48
    see also cultural mingling
Mennonites **7:***13–14;* **10:**25
    and cross-cultural dating **5:**52

dress **3:**52
    Paraguyan **8:**51
Menominee **7:**12
Mescalero **1:**26
mestizos **7:**17, 67; **8:**12; **9:**5
Mestrovic, Ivan **3:**16
Métis **4:**43; **5:**50; **7:***15–16,* 51; **9:**6
Mexicali, Chinese in **7:**19
Mexican-American War **7:**21
    and the Irish **7:**19
Mexican Farm Labor Program
    Agreement **3:**23
Mexican Revolution **7:**22
Mexicans **7:***21–25*
    see also Aztecs; Chicanos; Mayans;
        Mexico
    in the Alaskan fishing industry **3:**18
    crafts **3:**10
    discrimination against **1:**24
    families **4:***21–22*
    festivals **4:**24, 26, 38
    folklore **4:***38*
    labor unions **6:**40
    language **6:**59; **7:**24; **8:**14
    stereotypes **9:**9
    trades and professions **10:**36
    Zoot-Suit Riots **9:**7, 8; **10:**69
Mexico
    border **3:**21, *22,* 23–24, *26,* 30–31;
        5:30; **7:**21
    cultural borderlands **3:***30–31*
    emigration from **3:***21–26;* **7:**20
    illegal immigration from **3:**18, 21,
        23–25; *5:30, 34;* **7:**21, 23
    immigration **7:***17–20*
    literacy in **6:**61
    Native Americans **8:***6–7,* 12
    oil reserves **3:**25
    and World War I **10:**65
    Zapatista movement **7:**11; **8:**7, 15
Miami, Florida
    Brazilians **2:**5
    Cubans **3:**27, *29*
    Jamaicans **6:***18*
    Jews **6:**26
    Nicaraguans **8:**26
Michigan **10:**18
    Armenians **1:**37
    Bulgarians **2:**9
    Finns **4:***34*
    French **2:**31
    Native Americans, Northeast **7:**62
Micmac **2:**15; **7:**49, 61
Micronesia **8:**40
middlemen (sojourners) **9:**16
Middle Passage **9:**56
Midsommarfest **10:**24
migrant workers *see* workers, migrant
military, the, *see* war and military service
Miller, Dorie **10:**67
Mills, Billy **9:***54*
Milosevich, Slobodan **9:**46, 48
mining towns **5:**19
Minnesota **10:**18
    Czechs **3:***43*
    Finns **4:***34*
    Native Americans, Northeast **7:**62
Minority Health, Office of **4:**22
minstrel shows **9:***8*
Minuit, Peter **3:***54–55*
Miranda, Carmen **8:***61*
miscegenation **5:***51*
Mississippi **10:**18
    Native Americans, Southeast **7:***68*
Missouri **10:**18
Mixtecs **7:**17; **8:***6–7*
mobility, and cultural mingling **3:**34
Mohawks **6:**7; **7:**61, 62; **8:***8*
moieties **7:**46
mojados **3:**25
Molly Maguires **5:**65
Momaday, N. Scott **7:**58
Mongolians **7:**26

Montana **10:**18
    Blackfeet **1:**64, *65*
    Native Americans, Columbia
        Plateau **7:**53
    Native Americans, Great Plains **7:**59
Montcalm, Louis-Joseph de **3:***17*
Montenegrins **7:**27
    see also Serbians
Montezuma II **1:**56
Montreal
    African Canadians **1:**14
    Chinese population **2:**52
    cultural events **2:**35
Monument Valley, Arizona **8:***19*
Moody, Dwight Lyman **9:**10
Moran, George **9:***8*
Moreira, Airto **2:**6
Mormons **4:**50; **5:**28; **7:***28–29;* **9:**14
    and cross-cultural dating **5:**52
    polygamy **4:**21
Moroccans **8:***30–32, 34*
Morrill Act (1862) **3:**66
Morrison, Toni **6:**64
Morse, Samuel F.B. **8:***17;* **9:**34
mosques **1:**28
mountain men **4:**50
Mukherjee, Bharati **6:**64
multiculturalism **1:***48–49;* **7:***30–31*
    Canadian **2:**21; **7:***30–31*
Multiculturalism Act (1988; Canada) **7:**31
multiple ethnic origins **7:***32–33*
    see also intermarriage
Munro, Alice **6:**65
murals **4:***61;* **7:**25
music **7:***34–36*
    and African-Americans **1:***10, 12;* **4:**37
    bluegrass **7:**35
    blues **7:**34
    Cajun **2:***15,* 16
    Caribbean **6:**19
    classical **7:**35
    Conjunto **3:**31
    and cultural mingling **3:***35–36*
    Ecuadorian **3:**64
    folk **7:**35
    French-Canadian **2:**35
    gamelan orchestras **5:***45*
    gospel **1:***10;* **7:**34
    Hispanic **7:**36
    Hutterites and **5:**26
    Inuit **5:**57
    Irish **5:**69
    Jamaican **6:**19
    jazz **1:***12;* **2:**6, 40; **7:**34
    "Latino" **3:**40
    mariachi **7:**36
    Métis **7:**16
    Mexican **7:**25, 36
    Native American **7:**36
    norteño **7:**36
    Peruvian **8:***54,* 55
    politicized **3:**36
    polka **8:**60; **9:**63
    pop (popular) **4:**14; **7:**34
    Puerto Rican **8:**69
    rap **1:***12;* **3:**36
    rock-'n'-roll **7:**34, *36*
    Romanian **9:**23
    salsa **7:**36
    swing **7:**34
    zydeco **7:**35
Muslims **1:**28, 29; **7:***30*
    Azerbaijani **1:**53
    dress **3:**53
    Iranian **5:**60
    Iraqi **5:**61
    Pakistani **8:**43
    polygamy **4:**21
    and racism **9:**9
    Shi'ite **5:**60, 61
    Sunni **5:**61
    Turkish **10:**39, 41
Mutombo, Dikembe **2:***41*

Nader, Ralph **1:***30*
names
    personal **8:***52–53*
    place **6:**56; **10:**10
Napoleonic Wars **2:**26
Narváez, Pánfilo de **7:***18*
Nast, Thomas **8:**16
National Association for Bilingual
    Education (NABE) **6:**42
National Association for the
    Advancement of Colored People
    (NAACP) **1:***9–10;* **9:**9
National Broadcast Company (NBC) **2:**7
National Chicano Survey (NCS) **6:***59–60*
National Farm Workers Association **6:**40
National Football League **9:**69
National Health and Social Living
    Survey (1994) **5:**53
national loyalties **7:***37–38*
    see also cultural retention; language
        retention
National Origins Quota Act (1920) **2:**40
National Origins Quota Act (1924) *see*
    Immigration Act, of 1924
Nation of Islam **1:**11
Native American Association **8:**17
Native American Church **7:**60
Native American Religious Freedom
    Act (1978) **1:**27
Native Americans
    see also Aleuts; Apache; Aztecs;
        Blackfeet; Cherokee; Chippewa;
        Inuit; Mayans; native peoples;
        Navajo; Pueblo; reservation
        system; Tlingits
    in Alaska **4:**50; **7:***44–45*
    architecture **1:**31
    art **1:**39
    assimilation **1:***46,* 47–48; **3:**30, 38, 51,
        67; **6:**61; **7:**48; **8:**10; **9:**17
    in California **7:***46–48;* **8:**13
    in Canada **7:***49–51*
    in colonial America **3:**4
    Columbia Plateau **7:***52–54;* **8:**13
    crafts **3:***10–11*
    criminal gangs **3:**13
    dancing **7:**49
    displaced **4:**50
    dress **3:**51
    education **3:**67
    the English and **9:**6
    European culture imposed on **3:**30
    families **4:**23
    farmers **1:**15
    folklore **4:***36–37*
    Great Basin **7:***55–57;* **8:**13
    Great Plains **5:**18; **7:***58–60;* **8:**13
    housing **1:**26; **5:***18;* **6:**6; **7:**61, *63;* **8:**6;
        9:44
    intermarriage **5:**50
    languages **6:***42–45,* 55–58; **7:**47
    in literature **6:***63–64*
    medicine and healing **5:**13
    Menominee **7:**12
    Mexico's **8:***6–7,* 12
    music **7:**36
    newspapers **8:**23
    Northeast (Woodland peoples)
        7:*61–63;* **8:**13
    Northwest Coast **7:***64–66;* **8:**9, 13
    population statistics **8:**15
    religions **7:***63;* **9:**11
    sacred lands **8:**9, *10*
    segregation **9:**41
    Southeast **7:***67–69;* **8:***13,* 14
    Southwest and Mexico **8:***4–7, 13*
    Spanish conquistadors and **9:**5
    and state names **6:**56
    Sun Dance **7:**59
    taiko **7:**36
    treaties with **4:**49
    as U.S. citizens **9:**67
    women as religious leaders **9:**11

workers **6**:8; **8**:*8*
  and World War I **10**:55
  and World War II **10**:68–69
native peoples **8**:*12–15*
  and land rights **4**:50; **5**:11; **6**:7; **7**:46;
    8:*9–11*
nativism **8**:*16–18*
  see also prejudice, anti-immigrant
Naturalization Act
  of 1798 **5**:40; **8**:16
  of 1870 **6**:20–22
  of 1906 **5**:38
Navajo **1**:31; **4**:23; **8**:4, 14, *19–21*
  Code Talkers **6**:57; **10**:69
  language revitalization **6**:44
  and oil reserves **8**:6
  and the Rainbow Bridge **8**:*10*
  reservation (Navajo Nation) **8**:*19*; **9**:18
  rugmaking **3**:*11*
Navajo–U.S. Treaty (1868) **8**:21
neighborhoods, ethnic **1**:46
Nebraska **10**:18
  Czechs **3**:*43*
  Native Americans, Great Plains **7**:59
Nevada **10**:18
New Amsterdam **3**:5, *54*
New Brunswick, French Canadians **2**:31
New Deal **8**:21
New England **3**:5, 17
  French Canadians **2**:30, 33, *34*
  houses **1**:31; **5**:18
Newfoundland, English **2**:24
New France **2**:32, 33; **3**:17; **4**:43; **9**:4
New Glarus, Wisconsin **10**:26
New Hampshire **10**:18
New Jersey **10**:18
  Arab Americans **1**:*29*
  Chileans **2**:51
  Chinese **2**:53
  Colombians **2**:68
  Costa Ricans **3**:9
  Cubans **3**:28
  Dominicans **3**:*50*
  Dutch **3**:*64*
  Hondurans **5**:*17*
  Jews **6**:26
  Koreans **6**:34
  Nicaraguans **8**:27
  Paraguayans **8**:51
  Peruvians **8**:55
  Slovaks **9**:60
New Mexico **10**:18
  Native Americans, Southwest **8**:5
New Orleans, Louisiana **4**:43, *45*
  Congo Square **2**:40
  Jazz Festival **1**:*11*
  Mardi Gras **4**:24, *47*
Newroz **6**:37
New Spain **7**:18; **8**:4
newspapers and magazines **8**:*22–24*
New Sweden **10**:21
Newton, Huey P. **3**:*34*
New York City **2**:*64–65*
  see also Ellis Island
  African street vendors **10**:*62*
  Annual Turkish Day parade **2**:42, 44
  Arab Americans **1**:*29*
  Argentines **1**:*34*
  Armenians **1**:*37*
  Bangladeshis **1**:57, *58*
  Barbadians **1**:*59*
  Brazilians **2**:4, 5, 6
  Chinese **2**:*53*
  cultural mingling **3**:*31–32*
  Dutch **3**:*54–56*
  Ecuadoreans **3**:*63*
  ghettos **4**:*60*, 61
  Haitians **5**:*7–9*
  Jamaicans **6**:*18*
  Jews **6**:25, 26, 29
  Koreans **6**:34
  Little Italy **6**:*12*
  marriages outside ethnic groups **4**:*20*

Philippine Day Parade **4**:*30*
Puerto Ricans **8**:68
St. Patrick's Day Parade **4**:25; **7**:37
tenements **5**:*19*
Thanksgiving Day Parade **4**:26
New York State **10**:18
  African Americans **1**:6
  Bolivians **1**:*67*
  Chileans **2**:51
  Chinese **2**:52, *53*
  Colombians **2**:68
  Costa Ricans **3**:9
  Cubans **3**:28
  Czechs **3**:*43*
  Dominicans **3**:*50*
  Dutch **3**:*64*
  Finns **4**:*34*
  French **2**:31
  Guatemalans **4**:*67*
  Hondurans **5**:*17*
  Jews **6**:26
  Koreans **6**:34
  Native Americans, Northeast **7**:62
  Nicaraguans **8**:27
  Pacific Islanders **8**:*41*
  Panamanians **8**:*48*
  Paraguayans **8**:51
  Peruvians **8**:55
  Slovaks **9**:60
New Zealanders **8**:25
Nez Percé **7**:54; **8**:14
Nguyen, Dat **10**:*54*
Nicaraguans **8**:*26–29*; **9**:20
Nikolski **1**:19
Nisei Week celebrations **6**:*20*, 24
Nkrumah, Kwame **10**:*63*
Noriega, Manuel **8**:47
North Africans **8**:*30–35*
North Carolina **10**:18
  Cherokee **2**:49
  Native Americans, Southeast **7**:68
North Dakota **10**:18
  Native Americans, Great Plains **7**:59
North Star, Project **3**:17
Northwest Passage **5**:*56–57*
Norwegians **8**:*36–39*
Nova Scotia **2**:25, 32
  English **2**:*24*
  expulsion of Acadians from **2**:*13*
  Native Americans, Northeast **7**:62
Noxche (language) **2**:45
Nunavut **5**:58; **7**:31, 51; **8**:15

Oakland, California, Chinese **2**:*53*
Oath of Allegiance, U.S. **5**:38
occupations *see* industry and
    employment
Ohio **10**:18
  Amish population **1**:*22*
  Czechs **3**:*43*
  Finns **4**:*34*
  Slovaks **9**:60
oil reserves **3**:25; **8**:6
Ojibwa *see* Chippewa
Oklahoma **10**:18
  Cherokee **2**:49
  Native Americans, Great Plains **7**:59
  Native Americans, Southeast **7**:68
Oktoberfest **4**:54, *58*
Old Spanish Days fiesta **6**:*55*
Oliver, Frank **2**:20
Olmecs **7**:*17*; **8**:6, 7
Ontario
  see also Ottawa
  African Canadians in **1**:14
  English **2**:*24*
  Estonians in **4**:16
  French Canadians **2**:31
  Germans in **4**:*58*
  Jews **6**:26
  Native Americans, Northeast **7**:62
On the Road (Kerouac) **2**:35
Opium War **2**:54, *58*

Oregon **10**:18
  Finns **4**:*34*
  Native Americans, Columbia
    Plateau **7**:53
  Pacific Islanders **8**:*41*
  Treaty of (1846) **3**:18
Orthodox Church **4**:64; **9**:23
  Greek **4**:64
  in Protestant societies **9**:14
  Russian **9**:26
  Serbian **9**:46, 48
  Ukrainian **4**:5, 6
Osceola **9**:44, 45
Otavalo, Ecuador **3**:*63*, 64
Otay Mesa crossing **3**:*26*
"OTMs" illegal immigrants **3**:21
Ottawa, Ontario
  Parliament Building **7**:*39*
  tulip festival **3**:58
Ottoman Empire **1**:36; **8**:33; **10**:39

Pacific Islanders **8**:*40–42*
  see also Hawaiians; New Zealanders;
    Papua New Guineans
padrones **6**:*12–13*
Pahlavi, Mohammed Reza **5**:59
Paige, Rod **6**:*61*
paintings *see* art
Paiute **7**:55, 56
Pakistanis **8**:*43–44*
  see also Bangladeshis
Palestinians **1**:28; **8**:*45–46*
  see also Israelis
Palmer raids **8**:17
Panama Canal Treaty (1978) **8**:47
Panamanians **8**:*47–48*
Papineau, Louis-Joseph **9**:4
Papua New Guineans **8**:49
Paraguayans **8**:*50–51*
Parks, Rosa **9**:40, 41
Parti Québécois **6**:69
Pashtuns **1**:4
Peace Arch State Park **3**:20
Peace Maker **6**:6
Pearl Harbor **5**:31; **6**:22; **10**:67
Pella, Iowa **3**:56, *57–58*
Peña, Guillermo Gómez **3**:31
Penn, William **4**:11, 55; **9**:12
Pennsylvania **4**:11; **9**:12; **10**:18, 58
  see also Philadelphia
  Amish population **1**:22
  Dominicans **3**:*50*
  Jews **6**:26
  Slovaks **9**:60
Pennsylvania Dutch (Pennsylvania
    Germans) **4**:*57–58*
Pennsylvania Gazette, The **8**:22
Pensionado Act (1903) **4**:28
Perez, Hugo **9**:28
Persian Gulf War **5**:61
personal names **8**:*52–53*
Peruvians **8**:*54–55*
petroglyphs **1**:*39*
Peyotism **7**:60
Philadelphia, Pennsylvania **4**:*11*
  Jews **6**:26
  Mummers' Parade **4**:24
philanthropy, Greeks and **4**:62
Philippines, immigrants from, *see*
    Filipinos
Pilgrims, the **3**:4; **4**:9
piñatas **4**:*38*
Pinkster Day **2**:38
Pinochet, Augusto **2**:50, 51
Pittsburgh Agreement (1918) **9**:*59–61*
Pittsburgh, Pennsylvania, Croatians
    3:*14*, 15
Plains of Abraham, Battle of the **2**:32, 33
Plains people *see* Great Plains, Native
    Americans
Plantation of Ulster **9**:30
plantations **1**:7; **3**:5; **5**:48, 49; **9**:*56–57*
  in Hawaii **4**:28

Plessy v. Ferguson (1896) **1**:9; **3**:66; **9**:7
pluralism **9**:10
Plymouth, Massachusetts, colony **3**:4
poetry **6**:*62–63*
Poitier, Sidney **4**:32; **5**:52
Poland, origins of **8**:56
Poles **8**:*56–60*
politics
  English **4**:15
  Guatemalan **4**:67
  Guyanese **4**:68
  Haitian **5**:9
  Hondurans **5**:16
  the Irish and **5**:*68–69*; **7**:*4–5*
  the Italians and **6**:*15–16*
  Jamaican **6**:17
  Jews and **6**:31
  Koreans and **6**:36
  and lobbying **7**:38
  local politics (Canada) **6**:*68–69*
  local politics (U.S.) **7**:*4–5*
  "machine" **7**:4
  national politics (Canada) **7**:*39–40*
  national politics (U.S.) **7**:*41–43*
  Polish **8**:60
  and religion **7**:42; **9**:10
Polonia **8**:58
polygamy **4**:21; **7**:28, 29
Polynesia **8**:40
Portuguese **8**:*61–63*
Potawatomi **8**:9
potlatch **5**:6; **7**:66
  costume **7**:*64*
poverty **4**:*61*
Powell, Colin **1**:5
Prado, Perez Pantalon **3**:36
prejudice, anti-immigrant **1**:*23–24*; **3**:26;
    5:*32*
  see also discrimination; nativism;
    racial prejudice and racial theories
  against Arabs **1**:28
  against Filipinos **4**:29
  against Germans **6**:59; **8**:16, 18
  against the Irish **1**:23; **5**:41, 65; **8**:17
  against Italians **6**:*14*
  against Japanese **6**:*20–22*
  against Poles **8**:59
  against Ukrainians **10**:42
  against Vietnamese **10**:53
  in Canada **2**:21
  and diseases of immigrants **5**:13
  post-September 11, 2001 **5**:33
Presbyterians **9**:12
presidents, U.S. **7**:42
Presley, Elvis **7**:36
Prohibition **3**:23
Prohibition of the Slave Trade Act
    (1808) **10**:60
Proposition 187 **1**:24; **3**:26
Protestantism **9**:10, *12–13*
  evangelical Protestants **9**:14
  Germans and **4**:55, *57*
Provincetown, Massachusetts,
    Portuguese **8**:63
Prudhomme, Paul **2**:16
Pueblo **8**:6, 9, *64–65*
  Ancestral **8**:64
  Pueblo Revolt **8**:64; **9**:11
pueblos **1**:*31*
Puente, Tito **3**:41
Puerto Ricans **8**:*66–69*; **9**:66
  language **6**:61; **8**:67
  and *West Side Story* **7**:35
Pulitzer, Joseph **8**:23
Puritans **7**:42; **9**:12
Puzo, Mario **6**:64

Qaddafi, Muammar al- **8**:33
Quakers **3**:5; **9**:12
  see also Germantown
  colony for **4**:11
Quebec
  cultural events **2**:35

English Canadians **2**:25
French Canadians **2**:*19*, 21, *31*, 33
language **2**:*19*; **7**:31; **9**:*4*
separatism **2**:34; **6**:55, 69; **7**:40; **9**:*4*
and World War I **10**:64
Quebec City **2**:25, *26*, 35
Battle of the Plains of Abraham
(Battle of Quebec) **2**:32–33; **3**:*17*
early French colony **4**:*43*
Quebecois **6**:54, 55
Quiet Revolution **9**:4
quilting **1**:*40*; **3**:10
quince, los **1**:*33*
quinceaño **3**:*63*
quota system **5**:38–39, 43, 44

race riots
Chicago (1919) **2**:64
Los Angeles (1965) **2**:65
racial equality, in the military **10**:56
racial prejudice and racial theories **9**:5–9
see also Manifest Destiny; prejudice,
anti-immigrant
radio *see* broadcasting
railroad workers **2**:54; **4**:50; **9**:*49*; **10**:35
Rainbow Bridge, Utah **8**:*9, 10*
Rakcheyeva, Sabina **1**:*53*
Ramadan **1**:57
rancherias **7**:48
Rastafarians **6**:*19*
Reagan, Ronald **5**:*44*, 67; **8**:26
recessions, economic **5**:33
Reconstruction **1**:8
redemptioners **4**:56
Red River Resistance **7**:15
Red Scare **6**:14–15; **8**:18
Reform, War of the **7**:22
Refugee Escape Act (1960) **10**:8
Refugee Relief Act (1953) **2**:66; **10**:8
refugees *see* emigrés and refugees
refusniks **9**:27
Regulator movement **9**:32
religion **9**:10–14
see also Amish; Hutterites; Judaism;
Mormons; Muslims; Orthodox
Church; Protestantism; Roman
Catholicism
of African Americans **1**:11; **10**:63
Anabaptists **1**:21
of Arab Americans **1**:29
Buddhism **2**:*17*
Bulgarian Orthodox church **2**:9–10
and cultural mingling **3**:33
dress of religious groups **3**:51–53
of English Canadians **2**:28
Gypsies and **5**:4–5
Hawaiian **5**:11
Hinduism **1**:*44*; **5**:*20*; **9**:*13*
Hungarian **5**:*24*
and interfaith marriage **5**:52–53
Irish **5**:67–68
of the Iroquois **6**:6–7; **9**:11
Native American **6**:6–7; **7**:63; **9**:11
Peyotism **7**:60
politics and **7**:42; **9**:10
United Church of Canada **2**:28
repatriation **9**:15–16
see also deportation; returnees
reservation system **8**:6, 10; **9**:17–18
Apache reservations **1**:27
Blackfoot reservations **1**:65
California reservations **7**:47, 48
fractionalization **8**:10
Menominee reservations **7**:12
Sioux reservations **9**:52, 54
returnees **9**:19–20
see also repatriation
Revolutionary War *see* American
Revolution
Rhode Island **10**:18
Dominicans **3**:*50*
Ribaut, Jean **4**:*41*
Riel, Louis **7**:16; **9**:6

Rights and Freedoms, Charter of (1982;
Canada) **7**:31
Riis, Jacob **2**:65
Ringgold, Faith **1**:40
Roanoke Island **3**:4
rock carvings **1**:*39*
Rohani, Shardad **5**:*59*
Rojas, Arnold J. **6**:*64*
Roman Catholicism
see also Jesuits
Cajuns and **2**:16
Croatians and **3**:16
early **9**:12
and education **3**:65
the French and **4**:44–45
French Canadians and **2**:33
Maltese and **7**:8
Mexicans and **7**:*24*
Poles and **8**:59
in Protestant societies **9**:14
Salvadorans and **9**:29
Samuel Morse and **8**:17
Romanians **9**:21–23
Romany, (Gypsies) **5**:4–5
Roosevelt, Franklin D. **2**:7
Roosevelt, Theodore **6**:22
rootwork **5**:12
Rosh Hashanah **4**:25
Rush-Bagot Agreement (1818) **3**:*20*
Russians **9**:24–27
see also Cossacks; Soviet Union; Tatars
cultural identity **5**:36
Jews **5**:36; **7**:18; **9**:26
and Latvia **6**:49
Mennonites **7**:13

Sacco, Nicola **6**:14–15
Sadlirmiut **5**:57
Said, Edward **8**:46
St. Louis, Missouri, Pacific Islanders **8**:*41*
St. Lucy's Day **10**:24
St. Patrick's Day **5**:69
parades **4**:25; **5**:*69*; **7**:37
Saipan **8**:40
Salish **9**:41
Salt Lake City, Utah **7**:28
Pacific Islanders **8**:*41*
Salvadorans **9**:20, 28–29
Samoans **8**:40
Sandanistas **8**:26, 27
San Diego, California, Pacific Islanders
8:*41*
San Francisco, California **10**:17
African Cultural Festival **2**:41
Brazilians **2**:5
Chinatown **2**:52; **3**:*41*
Chinese **2**:53
Jews **6**:26
Koreans **6**:*34*
Pacific Islanders **8**:*41*
Santa Rosa, California, Scottish
Highland Games **3**:*53*
Saroyan, William **6**:64
Saund, Dilip Singh **9**:50
Schneider, Rob **4**:*29*
schools *see* education
Schwarzenegger, Arnold **1**:*51*
Scotch-Irish **9**:30–34
Scots **9**:35–39
Ulster *see* Scotch-Irish
Scottish Enlightenment **9**:38
sculptures **5**:*58*; **8**:28
Seattle, Washington, Pacific Islanders
8:*41*
Second Fort Laramie Treaty (1868) **9**:*17*,
54
Second Seminole War **9**:44
segregation and integration **1**:9, 10;
9:40–43
see also discrimination, anti-
immigrant; prejudice, anti-
immigrant
and housing **4**:61

Japanese **6**:20, 22, 23
segregation in education **3**:66; **6**:22;
9:41, 43
Seles, Monica **9**:48
Seminole and Creeks **9**:*44–45*
Creeks **7**:67, 68, 69; **9**:*44–45*
Seminole **7**:67, 68, 69; **9**:*45*
"separate-but-equal" doctrine **9**:7,
40–41
September 11, 2001, attacks **1**:4, 28; **3**:20;
5:40, 5:44; **10**:9
and the "axis of evil" **5**:60, 62
and border defenses **3**:19
and illegal immigrants **5**:30
immigrant harassment and dress **3**:53
and the INS **5**:39
prejudice and suspicion after **5**:33;
8:35
Sequoyah **2**:47
Serbians **9**:46–48; **10**:9
see also Montenegrins
Serbs, Bosnian **1**:68
Serra, Junipero **10**:*12, 13*
servants, indentured **1**:7; **9**:37, 38
shamans *see* medicine men
sharecroppers **1**:*15*, 16
Sharif, Omar **3**:*68*
Shaw, Bernard **2**:18
Shining Path **8**:54
shoe game, **8**:21
Shoshone **7**:55, *56*, 57; **8**:*11*
Sidhu, Sanjiv **5**:35
Sifton, Clifford **2**:20
"signcutting" **3**:19
Sikhs **3**:53; **9**:*49–50*
Sinatra, Frank **6**:*15*
Singaporeans **9**:*51*
see also Malaysians
Singer, Isaac Bashevis **6**:65
Sioux **5**:18; **7**:58, *60*; **8**:15; **9**:*17*, 52–54
slavery **9**:6–7, 55–58
African-American slaves **1**:*5, 7–8*, 11;
2:36, 38; **3**:5–6; **5**:31, 49; **6**:52; **8**:28
African-Canadian slaves **1**:13–14
East African **3**:*61–62*
freed **6**:52
names **8**:52, *53*
reparations for **9**:57
schools for ex-slaves **3**:66
slaves in the Caribbean **2**:36; **9**:55
slaves from the Caribbean **5**:31
Slavs **4**:*21*
South **10**:8–9
Slovaks **9**:59–62
see also Czechs
Slovenes **9**:*63–64*
Smart Border Declaration **3**:19
Smith, Alfred E. **7**:4
Smith, Jedediah **4**:50
Smith, Joseph **7**:28, 29
social mobility, and race **9**:65–69
sodbusters **5**:49
sod shanties **5**:18
sojourners (middlemen) **9**:16
Solidarity **8**:60
Solvang, California **3**:*45*, 48
Somalians **3**:59; **4**:6
Soriano, Edward **4**:27
South Africans **10**:*4*
South Carolina **10**:17, 18
anti-Irish prejudice **1**:23
Gullah people **3**:*10*
Native Americans, Southeast **7**:68
slaves **3**:5–6
South Dakota **10**:18
Native Americans, Great Plains **7**:59
Tribal Land Enterprise **8**:11
Wounded Knee **8**:15
Southern Africans **10**:5–7
South Slavs **10**:8–9
Soviet Union
see also Cold War; Russians
and Central Asia **2**:44

invasion of Chechnya **2**:45
Jews from **6**:29
Soyinka, Wole **8**:29
Spanish-American War **8**:66
Spanish Civil War **7**:19–20
Spanish Harlem (*el barrio*) **8**:68
Spanish language **6**:55, 59, 60; **7**:24
Spanish people **10**:*10–13*
see also Basques
early conquest by **7**:10, *18*; **8**:4, 64,
65; **9**:*5*
and Mexico **7**:17, 19–20
and racism **9**:5
sports **10**:*14–15*
African Americans and **1**:12; **9**:69;
10:*14–15*
baseball **8**:68; **9**:69; **10**:*14–15*
basketball **10**:14, 15
boxing **9**:69; **10**:*14*, 15
cricket **6**:19; **10**:14
diving **6**:36
English **4**:15; **10**:14
football **9**:69; **10**:15, 54
golf **7**:33
hockey **8**:*60*; **10**:14
hurling **5**:68
integration in **9**:*43*
lacrosse (stick ball) **7**:69
running **8**:*32*; **9**:*54*
soccer **6**:53; **9**:28; **10**:47
Thai boxing **10**:*30*, 31
Sri Lankans **10**:16
states, U.S. **10**:*17–18*
names **6**:56
Steerage Acts (1819) **5**:41
stereotypes **9**:9
of African-Americans **1**:*5*; **9**:*8*, 9
of Italian Americans **6**:14–15
of Poles **8**:59
of Russians **9**:27
Steuben Day parades **4**:58
stonecarving **3**:11; **5**:*58*
stores and storekeepers **10**:*19*
Stowe, Harriet Beecher **10**:58
Uncle Tom's Cabin **6**:62, 64; **10**:58
Strauss, Levi **5**:49
Stroessner Matiauda, Alfredo **8**:51
Stuyvesant, Peter **3**:*56*
subway, in Chicago **1**:68
summer camps **1**:*48*
Sun Dance **7**:59
Supreme Court
Canadian **7**:40
U.S. **7**:41, 43
Supreme Order of the Star-Spangled
Banner (Know-Nothings) **8**:17
Surinamese **10**:20
Susan Constant (ship) **4**:*9*
Suu Kyi, Aung San **2**:11
Swahili **3**:59
Swedes **5**:19; **9**:15; **10**:*21–24*
Swiss **10**:25–26
Syrians **10**:*27–28*
see also Palestinians

Taiwanese **2**:59, *60–61*
Tajikistan **2**:42
Taliban **1**:4
tamales **3**:8; 9
Tammany Hall **5**:65
Tan, Amy **6**:*64*
tango **1**:*35*
Tanzania **3**:60, 61
Tatars (Tartars) **10**:29
Taylor, Charles **6**:52
Tekesta **7**:67
television *see* broadcasting
Temporary Protective Status (TPS), for
Liberians **10**:5
tenements **4**:60; **5**:*19*
Tennessee **10**:18
Native Americans, Southeast **7**:*68*
tepees **5**:*18*; **6**:6

terrorist attacks
    see also September 11, 2001, attacks
    Libya and 8:33, 35
Tesla, Nikola 3:16
Teton (Lakota) 9:52
Texas 10:18
    Cajuns 2:15
    Chileans 2:51
    Chinese 2:53
    Colombians 2:68
    Costa Ricans 3:9
    Cubans 3:28
    Czechs 3:43
    French 2:31
    Guatemalans 4:67
    Hondurans 5:17
    Houston 9:34
    Koreans 6:34
    Nicaraguans 8:27
    Pacific Islanders 8:41
    Panamanians 8:48
    Paraguayans 8:51
Texas Rangers 3:21
Tex-Mex 3:31; 4:40; 7:24
textile industry 5:47
Thais 10:30–31
Thanksgiving Day 4:26, 40
Tibetans 4:7; 10:32
    Dalai Lama 4:7; 10:32
Tijerina, Reies López 7:24
Tippu Tip 3:61–62
Tlingits 5:6; 7:64, 65; 10:33–34
tobacco 5:48
To Kill a Mockingbird (Lee) 6:64
Toltecs 7:17; 8:6, 7
Tongans 8:40
"tongs," Chinese 3:12, 35
Toronto
    African Canadians 1:14
    Africans 9:66
    Bosnians in 1:69
    Chinese population 2:59
    English 2:24
    Jews 6:26
    local council 6:68–69
totem poles 7:44, 64, 66
trades and professions 3:10; 10:35–36
    see also industry and employment
    Venezuelans 10:50
Trail of Tears 2:49; 7:67, 69; 9:32
transnationalism 7:38
Tresca, Carlo 6:14
Trianon, Treaty of (1920) 5:23
Tribal Land Enterprise 8:11
Trinidadians and Tobagonians 10:37–38
Trudeau, Pierre 2:20, 21
Trujillo, Rafael 3:49
Truman, Harry S. 5:39; 6:23; 8:68
Tsimshians 7:44
Tunisians 8:34–35
Turchaninov, Ivan (John Turchin) 3:7

Turkey, see also Armenians
Turks 10:39–41
    see also Kurds
Turner, Nat 1:8; 9:57
Tuskegee Airmen 10:68
Twenty Years at Hull House (Addams)
    6:62

Uganda 3:61
Ukrainians 10:42–44
    see also Cossacks
    in Canada 2:20
    Orthodox Church 4:5, 6
    and World War I 10:42, 64
Ulster Scots see Scotch-Irish
Unangans see Aleuts
Uncle Tom's Cabin (Stowe) 6:62, 64; 10:58
Underground Railroad 1:13; 9:58
unions, labor 6:39–40
United Church of Canada 2:28
United Farm Workers union (UFW) 1:16
United Irishmen 9:32
United Nations, and refugees 4:4
Universal Negro Improvement
    Association (UNIA) 9:6
universities 3:65; 5:68
urban deprivation see ghettos
urban reform and race 10:45–46
Uruguayans 10:47–48
Utah 10:18
    Mormons 7:28
    Pacific Islanders 8:41
    Serbians 9:48
Ute 7:55, 56, 57

Vancouver
    African Canadians 1:14
    Chinese population 2:52, 59
Vanzetti, Bartolomeo 6:14–15
Vatra 1:18
Vegreville, Alberta 10:42
Velvet Revolution 9:61
Venezuelans 10:49–50
Vermont 10:18
Vesterheim Museum, Iowa 8:39
Vietnamese 4:6; 10:51–54
    Hmong women 3:10
Vietnam War 6:46
View of Boston (Cole) 1:39
Virginia 10:18
    Bolivians 1:67
    Native Americans, Northeast 7:62
    Pacific Islanders 8:41
    Paraguayans 8:51
    Peruvians 8:55
voodoo 5:7, 9, 13

Waldensians 6:11
Walesa, Lech 8:60
Walters, Barbara 2:8
war and military service 5:47; 10:55–56

war brides 1:50; 4:12; 10:57
War Measures Act (1914) 10:64
"war on terror" 1:4
War Relocation Authority 1:23
Warrior gangs 3:13
Washington, Booker T. 3:66
Washington, D.C.
    Bolivians 1:67
    Brazilians 2:5
    Jews 6:26
    Koreans 6:34
    March on 1:9; 9:41
    National Cathedral 3:11
    White House 7:41
Washington State 10:18
    Finns 4:34
    Japanese 6:21
    Native Americans, Columbia
        Plateau 7:53
    Native Americans, Northwest Coast
        7:65
    Pacific Islanders 8:41
Washoe 7:55, 56, 57
Weah, George 6:53
weaving 8:21
    basket 7:55
weddings
    see also marriage(s)
    Greek 4:64
    Hindu 1:44
    intermarriage 5:51
    Jewish 4:20
    Pacific Islanders 8:42
Welch, Raquel 1:66
Welsh 10:58–59
West Africans 10:60–63
    see also Liberians
Western Samoa 8:40
West Side Story (movie) 7:35
Wetback, Operation 3:25
West Virginia 10:18
whaling 5:57
White Buffalo, The (Catlin) 1:64
Whitman, Walt 6:63
Wiesel, Elie 6:65
wikiups 8:6
Wilson, Woodrow 9:33
Wisconsin 10:18
    Czechs 3:43
    Little Norway homestead 8:36
    Native Americans, Northeast 7:62
Witherspoon, John 9:38
Wolfe, James 2:25; 3:17
Woman Warrior, The (Kingston) 2:55
women
    see also war brides
    Hmong 6:47
    Iroquois 6:4–5; 9:11
    in local politics 6:69
    Macedonian 7:6
    Native American 7:60; 9:11

West African 10:60
Woods, Tiger 7:33
workers, migrant 3:25
    Bracero Program 3:23, 25; 7:20
    Filipino 4:27, 28
    Puerto Rican 8:68
Work, Hubert 8:9
World War I 10:64–66
    African Americans and 10:55, 66
    and Armenians 1:36, 38
    and black migration 1:9; 9:42
    Canada's role in 10:56, 64
    German Americans and 10:65
    and the German language 6:59
    Irish Americans and 10:65
    Native Americans and 10:55
    and Turks 10:39
    and Ukrainians 10:42, 64
World War II 10:67–69
    see also war brides
    African Americans 10:55–56, 68, 69
    British evacuees to Canada 2:26
    Canadians in 2:29; 10:68
    Estonian refugees 4:16
    and the French 4:45
    and the Italians 6:15
    and the Japanese 1:23; 2:20; 5:31, 33;
        6:22, 23, 56; 9:20
    and Jews 4:56
    Mexican Americans in 10:56, 67
    and Mexican labor 7:20, 23
    Native Americans and 6:57; 10:68–69
    Navajo Code Talkers 6:57
    Pearl Harbor 5:31
    Poles and 8:56–58
    postwar war brides 1:50; 2:26–27
    refugees from 2:66; 4:16; 5:39, 43;
        6:29, 48–49; 8:58; 9:26–27, 63
    Russian refugees 9:26–27
    and South Slavs 10:8
    and Ukrainians 10:42–43
Wounded Knee 8:15; 9:54
Wright, Carroll D. 2:33
Wyoming 10:18
    Native Americans, Great Plains 7:59

Yahi culture 7:48
Yakima 7:54
Yugoslavia, Federal Republic of 7:27
    see also Montenegrins; Serbians
Yugoslavia, former
    see also Macedonians
    national loyalty to 7:38
    refugees from 4:6
Yupiks 7:44

Zapatista movement 7:11; 8:7, 15
Zapotecs 7:17, 19; 8:6–7
Zimmerman Telegram 10:65
Zonians 8:47, 48
Zoot-Suit Riots 9:7, 8; 10:69

Picture credits

Front cover: Corbis: Joseph Sohm; **background image: Corbis:** Bettmann. **Corbis:** 67; James L. Amos 57; Tony Arruza 10, 29; Bettmann 5, 14, 16b, 17, 18, 21, 23, 27, 30,42, 49, 56, 58; Richard Cummins 45; Sandy Felsenthal 52; Kevin Fleming 11, 65; Philip Gould 8; Annie Griffiths Belt 19, 31; Gunter Marx Photography 16t, 20; Eric and David Hosking 62; Hulton-Deutsch 61; Dewitt Jones 53; Wolfgang Kaehler 63; Kelly-Mooney Photography 37; Beebe Morton 41; Joseph Sohm 4; Ted Streshinsky 48; Jas E. Taylor 66; David & Peter Turnley 59; Michael S. Yamashita 51; **Getty Images:** 32, 34, 38, 44, 54; Brooklyn Productions 33; Frank Driggs Collection 35; NBC TV 47; Howard Pyle 6; **Rex Features:** Action Press 40; Jeroen Oerlemans 39; Marc Sharratt 36; **Robert Hunt Library:** 12, 68; **U.S. Customs Service:** James R. Tourtelotte 22, 24, 26.